Sweet Vegan

Sweet Vegan

70 Delicious Dairy-Free Desserts

Emily Mainquist

Photography by Penny de los Santos

Kyle Books

Published in Great Britain in 2011 by
Kyle Books
23 Howland Street, London W1T 4AY
www.kylebooks.com

ISBN 978-0-85783-001-2

10 9 8 7 6 5 4 3 2

First published in United States of America 2011 by
Kyle Books
www.kylebooks.com

Text © 2011 Emily Mainquist
Photography © 2011 Penny de los Santos
Book design © 2011 Kyle Cathie Limited

Project editor Anja Schmidt
Angliciser Jo Richardson
Designer Rita Sowins/Sowins Design
Photographer Penny de los Santos
Food Styling Susan Vajaranat
Prop Styling Audrey Weppler
Copyeditor Helen Chin
Production Lisa Pinnell

Colour reproduction by Sang Choy International
Printed and bound in China by Toppan Leefung Printing Co, Ltd.

✳ Contents ✳

Thank you for picking up this book and for exploring the world of tasty vegan desserts. As Emily so wonderfully demonstrates, vegan sweets can be both delicious and easy to make. You'll love making and eating these treats, and you can feel good in knowing that animals were not made to suffer for your eating pleasure.

Sweet Vegan is an excellent contribution to a burgeoning food movement. It comes amidst growing evidence about how factory farming threatens human health, the environment and the well-being of animals. More and more people are changing how they eat. Restaurants and grocery stores across the UK, as in the USA, are offering a wide variety of vegan foods, and amazing cookbooks like Emily's *Sweet Vegan* are providing recipes and advice for people who want to cook or prepare raw dishes at home. People are rediscovering the art of food preparation and the joy that comes with creating and sharing tasty morsels with friends, family and loved ones. And the positive experience is enhanced when the food is cruelty-free.

As we think about our food choices and endeavour to live in a way that is humane, healthy and environmentally sustainable, we must inevitably move towards consuming plant foods in place of animal products. Alternatives to meat, dairy and eggs are hitting the marketplace, and chefs of all stripes are getting creative in the kitchen. In *Sweet Vegan*, Emily provides wonderful recipes for you to try along with helpful advice about plant-based substitutes for dairy and eggs.

It doesn't make sense to support a food system that causes unnecessary violence and environmental destruction, especially when there are healthy plant-based alternatives that can satisfy every gustatory desire. Emily has produced a wonderful book that shows how enjoyable vegan desserts can be, and in addition to satisfying your taste buds, the dishes included here will also sit well with your conscience.

—Gene Baur, Watkins Glen, New York, USA, August 2010

So Why Vegan?

If you've picked up this cookbook, you may be asking yourself why vegan? There are many reasons. Vegan means loving animals and, by not consuming any animal products, letting them live a healthy, enjoyable life on this earth just as we do. Vegan means taking care of the environment – all the transportation in the world combined doesn't equal the greenhouse gases produced by livestock on factory farms. And 70% of the grain grown in the USA is used to feed animals on factory farms, food that could go a long way to feeding starving people around the world. Vegan also means being healthy; when I made the switch, I felt better, had more energy and didn't need to worry about my weight or cholesterol. Being vegan is better for animals, the earth and ourselves!

Growing up in my Italian family, everything revolved around food. I didn't play games or watch TV like other kids my age. I was in the kitchen, baking with my mum: breads, cannoli, rum cake, peach biscuits and all kinds of Italian cookies. I remember standing on a chair when I was too short to reach the counter and measuring the flour and sugar for a batch of cookies. It was so exciting to see the results of my hard work and nothing beat eating the cookies fresh out of the oven. My mum was known for her desserts and loved to give them away to the postman, neighbours, the electrician that came by to fix some wires at her house – it didn't matter who they were, it was her joy to give people great-tasting desserts.

I share that passion for brightening someone's day with baked goods. My plan was to go to culinary school and become a pastry chef. I needed a portfolio to apply, so I started a 'business' out of my parents' house, putting menus for desserts in our neighbours' mailboxes. Soon I was getting orders from the local car dealerships and hair salons. People were enjoying my desserts so much, I decided to forego culinary school and figure out a way to establish and expand my business into a full-time job.

Turning Vegan

Meanwhile, it took an insensitive former boss to open my eyes to animal testing and factory farming. Like many people, I was ignorant to the fact that animals are treated cruelly for testing human products. When I came across what was done to animals by factory farming, I was so disgusted that I turned vegetarian that day and never looked back.

Becoming vegan took a little more time. It involved a whole new way of thinking about food. For me, like many vegans, cheese was the most difficult animal product to give up. But once I was able to convince myself that I didn't need cheese or butter or milk to make my food taste good, it was easy to go vegan. And now I don't miss those ingredients at all. There are so many substitutes that there really is no excuse not to use them.

Determined to stick to a new lifestyle, I decided to turn one of my cookie recipes vegan. I bought all the vegan ingredients I could find, and after several attempts, I brought my first batch of vegan cookies into work: Oatmeal Cherry Chocolate Pecan to be exact. It wasn't out of the ordinary for me to bring in goodies, and without telling anyone that the cookies were vegan, I gave them out throughout the office. Later I explained that the cookies didn't have any eggs or dairy in them and everyone was so surprised. No one could tell that the cookies were vegan. With these rave reviews, I realised that I may be on to something.

Founding Emily's Desserts

One of my co-workers, who was also vegetarian, took some of the cookies into a local natural foods store. The owner of the store loved the cookies and wanted to carry them. So the idea of a vegan Emily's Desserts was born. Never in my wildest dreams did I think about selling my desserts in a grocery store. Online maybe, but getting them to the mass market was just a dream come true. Since then I've opened my first retail kiosk and have

collaborated with a vegan wine supplier to pair my cupcakes with wine. Making vegan desserts has happily become my full-time job!

It's incredibly rewarding to see someone who is vegan, or someone who has a dairy or egg allergy, eat my desserts. I know how hard it is to find delicious desserts that are cruelty-free. I love seeing people's smiles of surprise at how good a vegan cookie, or cake, can taste. In the end, I did not go to culinary school, and you might say that's life throwing me a curve ball, but my life story has unfolded into exciting and unforeseen experiences and challenges. My story had to happen the way it did for me to become vegan and want to make a difference for vegan cooks everywhere. With *Sweet Vegan*, I prove that vegan is absolutely delectable – and better for you.

The easiest way to someone's heart is through food. Food is a universal language that everyone can relate to. *Sweet Vegan* will help you make delicious desserts to share with your friends and family. The recipes are no-fuss and I have included a list below of my favourite substitutions for dairy and eggs, all of which are available online or at your local health-food store.

You no longer have to sacrifice taste for what you believe in.

So why not vegan?

PREFERRED VEGAN PRODUCTS

Butter substitute: Pure® Soya or Sunflower

Egg replacer: Ener-G® Egg Replacer™

Dairy-free and gluten-free chocolate chips: D&D Dairy Free Chocolate Chips

Vegan marshmallows: Sweet Vegan Vanilla Marshmallows

Cream cheese substitute: Tofutti® Better Than Cream Cheese®

Sour cream substitute: Tofutti® Sour Cream

Whipped cream substitute: Soyatoo®

Evaporated cane juice (unprocessed sugar): Biona Organic Rapadura Whole Cane Sugar

GLUTEN-FREE FLOUR MIX

After many cupcake rocks and cakes that felt like bricks, I found a flour combination that makes fluffy and moist gluten-free cakes. This recipe is easily substituted in most recipes that call for plain flour.

 MAKES 450G

310g white rice flour
105g potato starch
40g tapioca starch
1½ teaspoons xanthan gum

Combine all the ingredients and store in an airtight container in the refrigerator for up to 90 days.

APPLE CRISPS

Apple crisps are a versatile sweet that can be used as a decoration for a dessert, a topping on a salad or snacked on right from the pan. A delicious and crunchy treat.

 MAKES 24

3 medium Granny Smith apples
70g organic icing sugar

1. Preheat the oven to 120°C/250°F/Gas Mark ½. Line a 25 x 38cm baking tray with foil.
2. Thinly slice the apples and dip them in the icing sugar. Place in the prepared baking tray and bake for 20–25 minutes, or until the apples are golden brown. Cool and store in an airtight container.

COCONUT WHIPPED CREAM

A very easy whipped cream substitute, this recipe has a light and creamy texture with a slight coconut flavour. Delicious as a topping for dessert or with fresh berries.

 MAKES 475ML

400ml can full-fat coconut milk
35–70g organic icing sugar

1. Store the can of coconut milk in the refrigerator at least 8 hours before use. Once chilled, open the can, making sure not to tilt it over. Remove the lid and scrape the top layer of the coconut fat from the milk layer. Place the coconut fat into a stand mixer. Whisk on a low speed for 20 seconds. Add the icing sugar and whisk on a high speed for 10 seconds. The mixture will be lumpy.
2. Place in the refrigerator to firm for 1 hour. Whisk with a large whisk until the lumps are removed. Serve immediately.

✳ Breakfast Sweets ✳

✳ RECIPE LIST ✳

GRANOLA

 MAKES 850G

This granola recipe is the best you will ever taste – just ask my grandmother. The coconut and cinnamon add a richness to the slightly sweet oats. Also delicious over soya yogurt with fresh fruit.

320g rolled oats

45g dried unsweetened shredded coconut

145g whole raw almonds

80g soft dark brown sugar

½ teaspoon salt

1 teaspoon ground cinnamon

60ml vegetable oil

60ml light agave nectar

1 teaspoon vanilla extract

245g raisins

1. Preheat the oven to 160°C/300°F/Gas Mark 2.
2. In a large bowl, mix together the oats, coconut, almonds, brown sugar, salt and cinnamon.
3. Heat the oil and agave nectar in a microwave-safe bowl in the microwave for 20 seconds. Pour over the oat mixture. Add the vanilla extract and stir until combined. Spread the granola over the base of a 23 x 33cm baking tin.
4. Bake for 40 minutes, stirring every 10 minutes. Place the tin on a wire rack, stir in the raisins and push the granola to one side of the tin while cooling. This will allow the granola to cool in large clusters. Keep the granola in an airtight container for up to 1 month.

BLUEBERRY MUFFINS

MAKES 8–10

The cinnamon in these muffins complements the blueberries and adds a depth of flavour to an otherwise basic recipe. Spread some vegan spread on the muffins fresh out of the oven – so delicious.

195g unbleached plain flour

130g evaporated cane juice

½ teaspoon ground cinnamon

2 teaspoons baking powder

½ teaspoon salt

80ml vegetable oil

80ml soya milk

3 teaspoons egg replacer, whisked with 4 tablespoons warm water

2 teaspoons vanilla extract

150g blueberries

1. Preheat the oven to 180°C/350°F/Gas Mark 4. Line 8–10 holes of a standard-sized muffin tin with paper cases.

2. In a large bowl, mix together the flour, cane juice, cinnamon, baking powder and salt. Add the oil, soya milk, egg replacer and vanilla extract and mix until well combined, then fold in the blueberries. The mixture will be very thick.

3. Scoop 4 tablespoons of the mixture into each paper case. Bake for 18–20 minutes, or until a wooden skewer inserted in the centre of a muffin comes out clean.

BANANA WALNUT MUFFINS

 MAKES 8

My husband loves these muffins so much that I make them for him at least three days a week for a mid-morning snack. It's all about taste combined with texture here: the sweet banana mixes with the hearty walnut crunch for a healthy breakfast that tastes like dessert!

260g unbleached plain flour

130g evaporated cane juice

1 teaspoon bicarbonate of soda

½ teaspoon salt

115g butter substitute

3 ripe bananas

3 teaspoons egg replacer, whisked with 4 tablespoons warm water

1 teaspoon vanilla extract

85g shelled walnuts, chopped

1. Preheat the oven to 180°C/350°F/Gas Mark 4. Line 8 holes of a standard-sized muffin tin with paper cases.

2. In a large bowl, mix together the flour, cane juice, bicarbonate of soda and salt.

3. Melt the butter substitute in a microwave-safe bowl in the microwave. Using a food processor or the back of a spoon, blend or mash the bananas until they are puréed. Add the melted butter substitute, bananas, egg replacer, vanilla extract and chopped walnuts to the large bowl and mix until well combined. The mixture will be very thick.

4. Scoop 4 tablespoons of the mixture into each paper case. Bake the muffins for 18–20 minutes, or until a wooden skewer inserted in the centre of a muffin comes out clean.

CINNAMON CRANBERRY MUFFINS

 MAKES 8

The flavour combination of this muffin is truly unique: the spice from the cinnamon mixed with the tartness of the cranberries will make your taste buds sing. Dab with vegan spread and sprinkle with cinnamon sugar for an extra-rich treat.

195g unbleached plain flour

130g evaporated cane juice

2 teaspoons ground cinnamon

2 teaspoons baking powder

½ teaspoon salt

80ml vegetable oil

80ml soya milk

3 teaspoons egg replacer, whisked with 4 tablespoons warm water

2 teaspoons vanilla extract

90g dried cranberries

1. Preheat the oven to 180°C/350°F/Gas Mark 4. Line 8 holes of a standard-sized muffin tin with paper cases.

2. In a large bowl, mix together the flour, cane juice, cinnamon, baking powder and salt. Add the oil, soya milk, egg replacer and vanilla extract and mix until well combined. Fold in the cranberries. The mixture will be very thick.

3. Scoop 4 tablespoons of the mixture into each paper case. Bake the muffins for 18–20 minutes, or until a wooden skewer inserted in the centre of a muffin comes out clean.

✳ *Gluten-Free* ✳ CHOCOLATE-CHIP COURGETTE BREAD SQUARES

✳ MAKES 8

When I was growing up, my Aunt Trisha would often make this sweet bread. Her secret was to add lots of chocolate chips. I've adapted her recipe to make it both vegan and gluten-free. This bread is still as moist and delicious as my Aunt Trisha's, and now everyone can enjoy it.

55g butter substitute, at room temperature

110g soft dark brown sugar

1 teaspoon vanilla extract

145g Gluten-Free Flour Mix (page 13)

1 teaspoon bicarbonate of soda

½ teaspoon salt

1 teaspoon ground cinnamon

60g shelled walnuts, chopped

180g finely shredded courgette, drained

1½ teaspoons egg replacer, whisked with 2 tablespoons warm water

90g dairy-free and gluten-free chocolate chips

1. Preheat the oven to 180°C/350°F/Gas Mark 4. Grease and flour a 20 x 20cm baking tin.

2. In a stand mixer, beat the butter substitute with the brown sugar and vanilla extract on a medium speed for about 2 minutes until light and fluffy. Stop and scrape down the side of bowl, then add the flour, bicarbonate of soda, salt, cinnamon, walnuts and courgette. Mix on a medium speed for 30 seconds. Stop and scrape down the side of the bowl. Add the egg replacer and chocolate chips and mix for another 30 seconds.

3. Spread the mixture over the base of the prepared baking tin. Bake for 25–30 minutes, or until a wooden skewer inserted in the centre comes out clean. Cool on a wire rack for at least 1 hour before cutting into squares.

MONKEY BREAD

Monkey Bread is like a compilation of mini pull-apart cinnamon buns. Some might remember this dessert from Girl Guide days. I remember making it as a kid with my mum on winter days when school was out due to snow. This is delicious served with chai tea or hazelnut coffee.

BUNS
780g unbleached plain flour
6 teaspoons baking powder
1½ teaspoons salt
170g butter substitute
540ml soya milk

CINNAMON DIPPING SAUCE
4 tablespoons ground cinnamon
340g evaporated cane juice
225g butter substitute
300g soft light brown sugar

GLAZE
140g organic icing sugar
2 tablespoons water

1. Preheat the oven to 180°C/350°F/Gas Mark 4.
2. FIRST MAKE THE BUNS. Using a stand mixer, combine the flour, baking powder and salt on a low speed. With the motor still running, add the butter substitute 1 tablespoon at a time, waiting 5 seconds after each addition, until a soft dough is formed. Add the soya milk and beat the mixture on a medium speed for about 20 seconds until a soft dough forms.
3. Mix together the cinnamon and cane juice in a small bowl and set aside. On a lightly floured work surface, roll out the dough until 2.5cm thick and cut into 2.5cm squares. Roll each square into a ball, then dip in the cinnamon sugar mixture. Place each ball in a tube or bundt cake tin, arranging in even layers, working up the side of the tin.
4. In a microwave-safe bowl, melt the butter substitute in the microwave for 1 minute, then stir until completely melted. Add the brown sugar and stir until combined. Pour over the cinnamon sugar buns in the tin.
5. Bake for 35–40 minutes until golden brown. Cool in the tin on a wire rack for 10 minutes. Invert the tin to release the Monkey Bread, then leave to cool for a further 30 minutes.
6. Meanwhile, beat together the icing sugar and water until combined. Drizzle over the cooled Monkey Bread before serving.

PEACH BISCUITS

 MAKES 10

My mum always made peach biscuits for summer barbecues when I was a kid. We picked peaches from a peach farm in Pennsylvania and, when we got home, I helped her cut the biscuits and dip them into the butter and cinnamon sugar. So delicious on a hot summer day, these biscuits are great served for brunch or dessert.

BISCUITS

260g unbleached plain flour

2 teaspoons baking powder

½ teaspoon salt

55g butter substitute

180ml soya milk

FRUIT TOPPING

4 large peaches

3 tablespoons apricot conserve or jam

1 tablespoon water

COATING

170g evaporated cane juice

2 teaspoons ground cinnamon

335g butter substitute

1. Preheat the oven to 190°C/375°F/Gas Mark 5.
2. FIRST MAKE THE BISCUITS. Using a stand mixer, combine the flour, baking powder and salt on a medium speed. With the motor still running, add the butter substitute 1 tablespoon at a time, waiting 5 seconds after each addition. Add the soya milk and beat the mixture on a medium speed until a soft dough has formed. Turn the dough out onto a lightly floured work surface and roll out until 1cm thick. Cut out biscuits with a 10cm round cutter. Re-roll the dough trimmings and cut out more biscuits. Set aside.
3. Wash and dry the peaches, then halve, discard the stones and cut into 5mm-thick slices. Set aside.
4. MAKE THE COATING. Mix together the cane juice and cinnamon in a medium bowl. Melt the butter substitute in a microwave-safe bowl in the microwave for 1 minute. Dip the biscuits into the melted butter, then in the cinnamon sugar and place on a 25 x 38cm baking tray.
5. Create a well in each biscuit. Arrange the sliced peaches, slightly overlapping, in each well. Sprinkle with any remaining cinnamon sugar.
6. Bake for 12–15 minutes, or until golden. Cool on a wire rack for 5 minutes. Meanwhile, melt the apricot conserve with the water in a microwave-safe dish in the microwave for 20 seconds, then spread onto the still-warm biscuits before serving.

CINNAMON CRUMB CAKE

 SERVES 12

This cake is definitely a classic that cried out for a yummy vegan version. The combination of moist yellow cake swirled with cinnamon and topped with a buttery brown sugar topping – how much better can it get? Cinnamon Crumb Cake is always fantastic with coffee and great conversation.

CRUMB TOPPING

130g unbleached plain flour

100g soft light brown sugar

1 teaspoon ground cinnamon

70g butter substitute

CAKE

225g butter substitute, at room temperature

255g evaporated cane juice

2 teaspoons vanilla extract

390g unbleached plain flour

4 teaspoons baking powder

2 tablespoons ground cinnamon

6 teaspoons egg replacer, whisked with 8 tablespoons warm water

240ml soya milk

1 tablespoon cider vinegar

Organic icing sugar, for sprinkling

1. Preheat the oven to 180°C/350°F/Gas Mark 4. Grease and flour a 23 x 33cm baking tin.

2. FIRST MAKE THE CRUMB TOPPING. In a stand mixer, combine the flour, brown sugar and cinnamon on a medium speed. With the motor still running, add the butter substitute 1 tablespoon at a time. Continue mixing until the topping resembles very coarse sand. Set aside.

3. Using a stand mixer, beat together the butter substitute, cane juice and vanilla extract until combined. Stop and scrape down the side of the bowl, then turn the mixer to a high speed and beat the mixture for about 2 minutes until it is light and fluffy.

4. In a small bowl, mix together the flour, baking powder and cinnamon. In a separate bowl, combine the egg replacer with the soya milk and vinegar. Alternate adding the dry and wet ingredients, starting and ending with the dry ingredients, to the mixer bowl. After each addition, beat for 10 seconds on a medium speed and stop and scrape down the side of bowl, making sure that all the butter substitute is incorporated. Beat for a further 30 seconds.

5. Spread the mixture into the prepared baking tin and sprinkle with all of the crumb topping. Bake the cake for 45–50 minutes, or until a wooden skewer inserted in the centre comes out clean. Sprinkle with icing sugar.

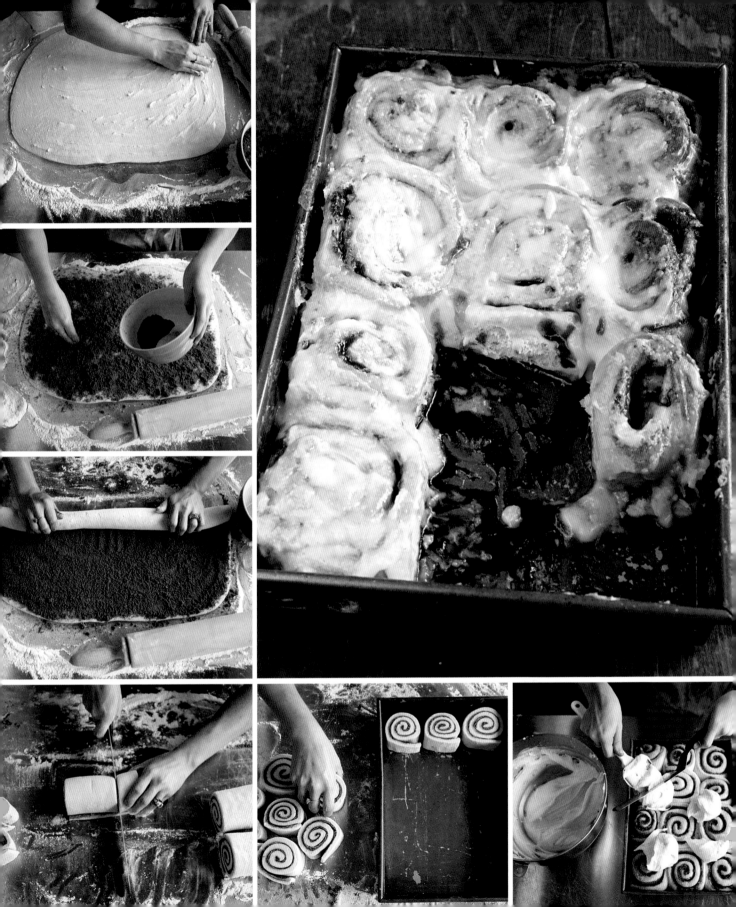

CINNAMON ROLLS

 MAKES 12

You will not be disappointed with this recipe. The rolls come out rich and gooey, just like the ones from your childhood. I sell these in stores and can't keep them on the shelves. Nothing is better on a weekend than the smell of cinnamon rolls in the morning.

DOUGH

240ml soya milk

2¼ teaspoons dried active yeast

3 teaspoons egg replacer, mixed with 4 tablespoons warm water

80g organic white sugar

630g strong white bread flour, plus extra for dusting

1 teaspoon fine sea salt

75g butter substitute, melted

FILLING

75g butter substitute, softened

160g soft dark brown sugar

2 teaspoons ground cinnamon

Cream Cheese Frosting (page 66)

1. Preheat the oven to 190°C/375°F/Gas Mark 5.
2. Warm the soya milk in the microwave for 30 seconds. Place the yeast in the bowl of a stand mixer, pour in the warm soya milk and leave the yeast to activate for about 10 minutes or until it has foamed. Add the egg replacer, sugar, flour, sea salt and melted butter substitute to the bowl. With a dough hook, mix on a medium speed until combined and a dough ball has formed. Continue to mix for a further 30 seconds to knead the dough. Place the dough in a lightly greased large stainless-steel bowl or plastic container and cover with cling film or a tea towel. Leave in a warm place to rise for at least 30 minutes, or until doubled in size.
3. Once the dough has risen, lightly flour your work surface and rolling pin. Roll the dough into a 40 x 51cm rectangle. Spread the softened butter substitute in a layer on top, then evenly sprinkle with the brown sugar and cinnamon. Roll the dough up lengthways as tightly as possible. Using a serrated knife, cut the long roll into 12 even rolls. Place the rolls in a 23 x 33cm baking tin. Cover again and leave to rise until doubled in size.
4. Bake the cinnamon rolls for 12–14 minutes or until slightly golden. Spread with the Cream Cheese Frosting and serve immediately, or store covered at room temperature and reheat in the microwave for 20–30 seconds for a fresh out-of-the-oven taste.

PUMPKIN ROLL

This dessert has always been a classic at our house in the autumn. A perfect addition to your dinner party table, it's also great served with spiced cider.

100g unbleached plain flour

170g evaporated cane juice

1 teaspoon bicarbonate of soda

¾ teaspoon ground cinnamon

4½ teaspoons egg replacer, whisked with 6 tablespoons warm water

165g pumpkin purée

70g organic icing sugar

CREAM CHEESE FILLING

85g butter substitute, at room temperature

225g tofu cream cheese, at room temperature

1 teaspoon vanilla extract

420g organic icing sugar, plus 2 tablespoons for dusting

1. Preheat the oven to 180°C/350°F/Gas Mark 4. Grease and flour a 25 x 38cm Swiss roll tin or baking tray.

2. Using a stand mixer, combine the flour, cane juice, bicarbonate of soda and cinnamon. Add the egg replacer and pumpkin and beat for 30 seconds on a medium speed. Spread over the prepared tin.

3. Bake for 10–12 minutes, or until a wooden skewer inserted in the centre of the cakes comes out clean. Flip the cake out onto a piece of greaseproof paper that has been sprinkled with the icing sugar. Roll the cake and greaseproof paper together widthways as for a Swiss roll. Leave to cool for 30 minutes.

4. MEANWHILE, MAKE THE CREAM CHEESE FILLING. In a stand mixer, beat the butter substitute and cream cheese at a medium speed for about 2 minutes until smooth. Stop and scrape down the side of the bowl. Add the vanilla extract and mix on a medium speed for 20 seconds. With the motor still running, add the main quantity of icing sugar a third at a time, stopping and scraping down the side of the bowl after each addition. Whip the filling for a further 1 minute on a high speed.

5. Unroll the cooked pumpkin cake and spread the filling evenly on top. Re-roll the cake without the towel and refrigerate for 2 hours before serving. Dust with the remaining 2 tablespoons icing sugar just before serving.

✹ Sweets in Crusts ✹

✳ RECIPE LIST ✳

DUTCH APPLE PIE

 SERVES 8–10

> Dutch apple pie has been around for centuries – probably because everyone loves the flavourings of cinnamon and lemon juice with the tart apples. Dutch apple pies are traditionally finished with a crisp lattice top, but I like to use a sweet crumb topping.

CRUST

75g non-hydrogenated vegetable margarine
165g unbleached plain flour
¼ teaspoon salt
4 tablespoons cold water

APPLE FILLING

6 large Granny Smith apples
35g unbleached plain flour
130g evaporated cane juice
2 teaspoons ground cinnamon

CRUMB TOPPING

130g unbleached plain flour
100g soft light brown sugar
70g butter substitute

1. Preheat the oven to 220°/425°F/Gas Mark 7.

2. MAKE THE CRUST. Using a stand mixer, beat the margarine on a medium speed until smooth. Scrape down the side of the bowl and add the flour and salt. While the motor is still running, add the cold water 1 tablespoon at a time until a dough starts to form. Continue mixing for about 20 seconds until just combined (over-mixing will make the dough tough). On a lightly floured work surface, roll out the dough until 5mm thick. Roll the dough around a rolling pin and unroll it into a pie plate or tart dish. Trim the extra dough and crimp the edge. Set aside.

3. MAKE THE APPLE FILLING. Peel, core and thinly slice the apples 5mm thick. In a large bowl, mix the flour, cane juice and cinnamon with the apple slices. Set aside.

4. MAKE THE CRUMB TOPPING. Using the mixer, combine the flour and brown sugar. While the motor is still running, add the butter substitute 1 tablespoon at a time. Mix until the crumb topping resembles very coarse sand.

5. Spoon the apple filling into the pie crust, making sure not to get the liquid from the bowl into the pie crust (this will help the pie to stay together once cut). Top with all of the crumb topping. Place the pie plate or tart dish on a foil-lined baking sheet for easy cleaning. Cover the pie with foil and bake for 40 minutes. Turn down the heat to 180°C/350°F/Gas Mark 4, remove the foil and bake for a further 10 minutes to brown the topping and crust. Leave to cool on a wire rack for 1 hour. Lightly cover at room temperature to store.

APPLE CHEESECAKE TART

This dessert is a combination of cheesecake and apple pie – and a unique result of one of my brainstorming sessions. It is a delicious mix of smooth vanilla filling and crisp cinnamon apples. I love to add the beautiful garnish of apple crisps; the recipe can be found at the end of the introduction to this book.

CRUST

75g non-hydrogenated vegetable margarine

180g unbleached plain flour

¼ teaspoon salt

4 tablespoons cold water

CHEESECAKE FILLING

225g tofu cream cheese, at room temperature

155g tofu sour cream

60g evaporated cane juice

1 teaspoon vanilla extract

1½ teaspoons egg replacer, whisked with 2 tablespoons warm water

1. Preheat the oven to 180°C/350°F./Gas Mark 4.

2. FIRST MAKE THE CRUST. Using a stand mixer, beat the margarine on a medium speed until smooth. Add the flour and salt and mix for about 20 seconds until combined. Add the cold water 1 tablespoon at a time, mixing after each addition. Continue mixing for about 30 seconds until a soft dough is formed (over-mixing will make the dough tough). On a lightly floured work surface, roll out the dough until 5mm thick. Prick all over with a fork. Roll the dough around a rolling pin and then unroll into a 23cm tart dish. Press against the base and side of the dish, trimming any extra dough. Bake for 15 minutes, then remove from the oven and set aside.

3. MEANWHILE, MAKE THE CHEESECAKE FILLING. Using the mixer, beat the cream cheese on a medium-high speed until smooth. Stop and scrape down the side of the bowl, then add the sour cream, cane juice and vanilla extract to the bowl. Mix the filling on a medium speed for about 1 minute, stopping and scraping down the side of the bowl as necessary. Add the egg replacer to the mixing bowl and beat for a further 30 seconds on a high speed. Spread the mixture evenly into the cooled pastry crust.

4. To make the apple filling, peel, core and slice the apples 5mm thick. In a medium bowl, mix the apples with the cane juice and cinnamon. Arrange the apples on top of the cheesecake filling in a single layer.

APPLE FILLING

3 medium Granny Smith apples

45g evaporated cane juice

1 teaspoon ground cinnamon

CRUMB TOPPING

130g unbleached plain flour

50g organic soft light brown sugar

40g shelled pecan nuts, chopped

70g butter substitute

APPLE CRISPS, for decorating
(page 13)

8–10 cinnamon sticks

5. MAKE THE CRUMB TOPPING. Using the mixer, combine the flour, sugar and pecan nuts. With the motor running on a medium speed, add the butter substitute in 1 tablespoon additions, waiting 10 seconds between each addition. Continue beating for about 30 seconds until the mixture resembles coarse sand, but watch closely to avoid the topping turning into one large clump. Sprinkle the crumb topping over the apples.

6. Bake the tart for 40–45 minutes until golden brown. Leave to cool, then refrigerate for at least 3 hours before cutting. Decorate each slice with an Apple Crisp and a cinnamon stick. Store any leftover tart in the refrigerator for up to a week.

APPLE CRISP

> I include dried cherries in this beloved dessert to add a slightly tart burst of flavour to the sweet apple cinnamon filling. I always use Granny Smith apples because they keep their crisp texture.

APPLE FILLING

6 Granny Smith apples
35g unbleached plain flour
130g evaporated cane juice
160g rolled oats
2 teaspoons ground cinnamon
120g dried cherries

CRUMB TOPPING

130g unbleached plain flour
80g soft dark brown sugar
70g butter substitute

1. Preheat the oven to 220°C/425°F/Gas Mark 7.
2. MAKE THE APPLE FILLING. Peel, core and thinly slice the apples 5mm thick. In a large bowl, mix together the flour, cane juice, oats, cinnamon and cherries. Add the apple slices and toss well. Set aside.
3. NEXT MAKE THE CRUMB TOPPING. In a stand mixer, combine the flour and brown sugar on a medium speed. With the motor still running, add the butter substitute 1 tablespoon at a time. Continue mixing until the topping resembles very coarse sand.
4. Spoon the apple filling into a 2-litre baking dish. Top with the crumb topping. Place the dish on a foil-covered baking sheet, for easy cleaning, and cover the baking dish with foil.
5. Bake the apple crisp for 40 minutes. Remove the foil, reduce the heat to 180°C/350°F/Gas Mark 4 and bake for a further 10 minutes, until the topping is nicely browned.

RUSTIC APPLE PIE

The overhanging and then folded-over crust for this pie gives it its rustic feel – not only a beautiful dish for the autumn but an easy and delicious recipe for an abundance of apples for picking.

CRUST

115g tofu cream cheese,
at room temperature

115g butter substitute,
at room temperature

195g unbleached plain flour

FILLING

115g tofu cream cheese,
at room temperature

3 tablespoons evaporated
cane juice

1¼ teaspoons ground cinnamon

2 medium Granny Smith apples,
peeled, cored and cut into 5mm
slices

1 teaspoon cornflower

60g organic dried cranberries

GLAZE

140g organic icing sugar

2 tablespoons water

1. Preheat the oven to 200°C/400°F/Gas Mark 6. Line a baking sheet with foil.

2. FIRST MAKE THE CRUST. Using a stand mixer, mix together the cream cheese and butter substitute on a medium speed for 2 minutes. Stop and scrape down the side of the bowl. Add the flour and mix until well blended. Shape the dough into a ball, wrap tightly with cling film and refrigerate for 1 hour. Once chilled, place the dough on a lightly floured work surface. Roll out into a 35 x 20cm rectangle, transfer to the prepared baking sheet and set aside.

3. NEXT MAKE THE FILLING. In a medium bowl, stir the cream cheese with 1 tablespoon of the cane juice and ½ teaspoon of the cinnamon. Mix until combined. Spread onto the crust within 5cm of the edge.

4. In another bowl, toss the apple slices with the remaining 2 tablespoons sugar, ¾ teaspoon of the remaining cinnamon and the cornflower. Arrange on top of the cream cheese filling in a single layer. Fold the edges of the pastry in towards the apples. Bake for 30–35 minutes, until the crust is golden.

5. Meanwhile, in a small bowl, beat together the icing sugar and water until combined. Set aside.

6. Remove the pie from the oven and sprinkle the dried cranberries on top while it's hot, then leave to cool for 15 minutes. Drizzle with the glaze.

STRAWBERRY CHEESECAKE

 SERVES 12–15

The crust made from my own agave digestive biscuit recipe gives this strawberry cheesecake an added wow factor. You can easily substitute blueberries, peaches or raspberries for the strawberries.

CRUST

24 Agave Digestive Biscuits
(page 104)

55g butter substitute, melted

45g evaporated cane juice

FILLING

900g tofu cream cheese

6 teaspoons egg replacer, whisked
with 8 tablespoons warm water

255g evaporated cane juice

340g strawberry jam

170g hulled strawberries, sliced

1. Preheat the oven to 180°C/350°F/Gas Mark 4. Grease and flour a 23 x 33cm baking tin.
2. FIRST MAKE THE CRUST. Using a food processor, finely crush the digestive biscuits.
3. In a medium bowl, combine the butter substitute, biscuit crumbs and cane juice. Press into the prepared baking tin and set aside.
4. NEXT MAKE THE FILLING. Using a stand mixer, beat the cream cheese on a medium speed for about 2 minutes until smooth, stopping and scraping down the side of the bowl as needed. Add the egg replacer and cane juice and blend on a medium-high speed for 2 minutes. Pour into the biscuit crust.
5. Bake for 40–45 minutes, until the centre is slightly firm. Refrigerate for 8 hours or overnight.
6. Before serving, spread the strawberry jam onto the cheesecake and top with the sliced strawberries.

TRIPLE CHOCOLATE CHEESECAKE

 SERVES 8–10

This cheesecake is a chocoholic's dream. Crisp chocolate cookie crust, rich chocolate filling and decadent chocolate ganache topping make up these three layers of chocolate bliss. This is extra delicious served with fresh berries.

CRUST

10 dairy-free chocolate sandwich biscuits

½ teaspoon ground coffee

40g butter substitute, melted

FILLING

225g tofu cream cheese, at room temperature

115g evaporated cane juice

115g tofu sour cream

3 teaspoons egg replacer, whisked with 4 tablespoons warm water

225g dairy-free and gluten-free chocolate chips

CHOCOLATE GLAZE

115g dairy-free and gluten-free chocolate chips

25g butter substitute

1 teaspoon light agave nectar

2 tablespoons tofu sour cream

Fresh raspberries and raspberry leaves, for decorating (optional)

1. Preheat the oven to 180°C/350°F/Gas Mark 4.

2. MAKE THE CRUST. Finely crush the sandwich biscuits in a food processor for about 1 minute. Pour into a medium bowl and add the ground coffee. Stir in the melted butter substitute. Press the crust into a 23cm disposable pie plate.

3. MAKE THE FILLING. Using a stand mixer, beat the cream cheese until smooth, stopping and scraping down the side of the bowl as needed. Add the cane juice and sour cream and mix for 1 minute on a medium speed. Add the egg replacer and mix for 30 seconds. Stop and scrape down the side and base of the bowl.

4. In a microwave-safe bowl, melt the chocolate in the microwave for 1 minute, stirring after 30 seconds. Remove from the microwave and stir until completely melted. Pour the chocolate into the mixing bowl while the motor is running, then blend on a high speed for 1 minute. Pour into the crust.

5. Bake for 25–30 minutes, until the filling slightly puffs around the edge and the centre is slightly firm. Cool on a wire rack for 30 minutes. Once cooled, remove the disposable pie plate and place the cheesecake on a serving dish.

6. MEANWHILE, MAKE THE GLAZE. In a microwave-safe bowl, melt the chocolate and butter substitute in a microwave for about 1 minute. Add the agave nectar and sour cream and stir until combined. Pour over the cooled cheesecake. Decorate with raspberries and raspberry leaves, if you like. Refrigerate for at least 4 hours before serving.

PUMPKIN PIE

 SERVES 8–10

I turned this recipe vegan by using coconut milk, which is very similar in thickness to evaporated milk. It is a great substitute and lends a creamy texture that is delicious.

CRUST

75g non-hydrogenated vegetable margarine

165g unbleached plain flour

¼ teaspoon salt

4 tablespoons cold water

PUMPKIN FILLING

425g can pumpkin purée

400ml can coconut milk

130g evaporated cane juice

2 teaspoons ground cinnamon

½ teaspoon salt

1 teaspoon xanthan gum

3 teaspoons egg replacer

1. Preheat the oven to 200°C/400°F/Gas Mark 6.
2. FIRST MAKE THE CRUST. Using a stand mixer, beat the margarine on a medium speed for about 10 seconds until smooth. Add the flour and salt and mix for about 30 seconds until combined. While the motor is still running, add the cold water 1 tablespoon at a time, then continue mixing for about a further 30 seconds until just combined (over-mixing will make the dough tough).
3. Turn the dough out onto a floured work surface. Using a floured rolling pin, roll the dough out until 5mm thick. Roll the dough around a rolling pin and unroll it into a pie plate. Trim the extra dough and crimp the edge. Set aside.
4. MAKE THE PUMPKIN FILLING. In a large bowl, mix together the pumpkin purée and coconut milk until combined. Add the cane juice, cinnamon, salt, xanthan gum and egg replacer, then mix together until well combined. Pour into the crust.
5. Bake for 40 minutes or until the centre of the pie is slightly firm. Cool in the pie plate for 30 minutes on a wire rack, then refrigerate for 8 hours or overnight before serving.

FRESH BERRY PIE

 SERVES 8–10

This simple dessert is perfect for a summer barbecue when berries are in season. A light drizzle of agave gives the berries a little extra sweetness. Garnish with fresh mint and Coconut Whipped Cream (see page 13). The simple crust is used again in the recipes for Fruit Pockets (see opposite) and Fruit Pizza (see page 54).

CRUST

75g non-hydrogenated vegetable margarine

180g unbleached plain flour

¼ teaspoon salt

4 tablespoons cold water

BERRY FILLING

290g blackberries

370g blueberries

245g raspberries

720g hulled strawberries

4 tablespoons light agave nectar

1. Preheat the oven to 220°C/425°F/ Gas Mark 7. Wrap the outside of a pie plate with enough foil to create an edge that is higher than the pie plate.

2. Using a stand mixer, beat the margarine on a medium speed for about 10 seconds until smooth. Add the flour and salt, and mix for about 30 seconds until combined. Add the cold water 1 tablespoon at a time, mixing for 10 seconds after each addition. Continue mixing for a further 30 seconds until just combined (over-mixing will make the dough tough).

3. Turn the dough out on a lightly floured work surface. With a lightly floured rolling pin, roll out the dough until 5mm thick. Prick all over with a fork. Roll the dough around the rolling pin and unroll it into the pie plate. Form the dough up the side of the pie plate and foil. This will allow for an abstract pie shell.

4. Bake the crust for 15 minutes, then leave to cool on a wire rack.

5. MEANWHILE, MAKE THE BERRY FILLING. Wash and dry the fruit. Cut some strawberries in half while leaving some whole. Gently stir all the fruit with the agave nectar in a large bowl. Spoon the mixture into the cooled pie crust and serve immediately.

FRUIT PARCELS

These delicious parcels are easy to take with you to a dinner party as a gift for your host. Make them for a picnic dessert or pack them in your children's lunchboxes for a healthier dessert at school.

CRUST
75g non-hydrogenated vegetable margarine
180g unbleached plain flour
¼ teaspoon salt
4 tablespoons cold water

FRUIT FILLING
2 small apples, peeled and cored
145g hulled strawberries, rinsed
75g blueberries, rinsed
6 tablespoons evaporated cane juice
100g unbleached plain flour

GLAZE
140g organic icing sugar
2 tablespoons water

1. Preheat the oven to 220°C/425°F/Gas Mark 7.
2. FIRST MAKE THE CRUST. Using a stand mixer, beat the margarine on a medium speed for 10 seconds until smooth. Add the flour and salt and mix for about 30 seconds until combined. With the motor still running, add the cold water 1 tablespoon at a time until a soft dough is formed. Continue to mix for about 30 seconds until just combined (over-mixing will make the dough tough). Roll out the dough on a lightly floured work surface until 5mm thick and cut out rounds with a 10cm round cutter. Re-roll the dough trimmings and cut out more rounds. Set aside.
3. MAKE THE FRUIT FILLING. Finely chop the apples and strawberries. Cut the blueberries in half. Mix each fruit in a separate bowl with a third of the flour and 2 tablespoons of the cane juice. Spoon 1 tablespoon of the fruit mixture onto the bottom half of each round of dough. Brush the edges of each dough round with water and fold the top half over the filling. Crimp the edges of the dough with the tines of a fork and cut 2 slits at the top of each parcel – this will allow the steam to escape.
4. Bake for 12–15 minutes, or until browned around the edges. Cool on wire racks for 30 minutes.
5. Meanwhile, make the glaze by beating together the icing sugar and water until combined. Pour over each fruit parcel before serving.

FRUIT PIZZA

 SERVES 6–8

Fresh fruit in season is the key to this dessert – and you can use any combination you like. Drizzle with melted chocolate or sprinkle with icing sugar for an extra sweetness factor.

CRUST

75g non-hydrogenated vegetable margarine

180g unbleached plain flour

¼ teaspoon salt

4 tablespoons cold water

CREAM CHEESE FILLING

40g butter substitute, at room temperature

115g tofu cream cheese

210–280g organic icing sugar (depending on how thick you want your filling)

1 teaspoon vanilla extract

FRUIT TOPPING

1 kiwi, peeled

6 strawberries, hulled

1 large peach, halved and stoned

13 blackberries

7 blueberries

7 raspberries

2 tablespoons apricot conserve or jam, melted

1. Preheat the oven to 190°C/375°F/Gas Mark 5.

2. MAKE THE CRUST. Using a stand mixer, beat the margarine on a medium speed for about 10 seconds until smooth. Stop and scrape down the side of the bowl. Add the flour and salt and mix on a medium speed for about 30 seconds until combined. Add the cold water 1 tablespoon at a time, mixing for 10 seconds after each addition. Mix for a further 30 seconds until just combined (over-mixing will make the dough tough). Roll the dough out on a lightly floured work surface into a rectangle 5mm thick. Prick all over with a fork and place on a pizza stone or baking sheet. Bake for 12–15 minutes, until lightly golden. Cool on a wire rack.

3. MEANWHILE, MAKE THE FILLING. Using the mixer, beat the butter substitute on a medium-high speed for about 1 minute until smooth. Stop and scrape down the side of bowl. Add the cream cheese and mix on a medium speed for about 1 minute until combined. With the motor still running, slowly add the icing sugar. Add the vanilla extract and beat for 1 minute on a high speed. Spread evenly over the cooled crust.

4. MAKE THE FRUIT TOPPING. Cut the kiwi fruit, strawberries and peach into slices 5mm thick. Arrange the fruit slices, overlapping, on top of the cream cheese filling with the berries. Brush the top of the fruit with the melted apricot conserve for a glossy finish. Store in the refrigerator for up to 2 days.

VARIATION

To make six 10cm tarts instead of a pizza, in step 2, after rolling the dough out 5mm thick, cut out six 10cm rounds. Place each round in a 5mm tart tin and bake and cool as instructed above. Continue preparing the filling and fruit, then when assembling, divide the filling between the cooled tart crusts and top with a fruit of your choice. You can mix the fruits or keep them uniform on each tart.

CHOCOLATE CHIP COOKIE CHEESECAKE

 SERVES 8–10

Two layers of rich chocolate chip cookie, a smooth
vanilla cheesecake filling plus a layer of chocolate make this
dessert so decadent. My Aunt Maria made this dessert when
I was young and it has always been one of my favourites.

COOKIE CRUST

Three 350g packets vegan cookie
dough

CHEESECAKE FILLING

675g tofu cream cheese, at room
temperature

130g evaporated cane juice

4½ teaspoons egg replacer, whisked
with 6 tablespoons warm water

1 teaspoon vanilla extract

Tempered chocolate, for decorating
(page 132)

1. Preheat the oven to 160°C/325°F/Gas Mark 3 if using a dark springform
   tin, 180°C/350°F/Gas Mark 4 if using a silver springform pan.

2. FIRST MAKE THE CRUST. Divide the dough into 2 equal amounts. Place a
   large piece of cling film on top of the springform tin base. Press half of
   the dough into the shape of the tin. Fold the cling film around the cookie
   dough and flip the tin base over to release the dough. Repeat with the
   remaining cookie dough, then place both cling film-wrapped rounds of
   dough in the freezer for 15 minutes.

3. NEXT MAKE THE CHEESECAKE FILLING. Using a stand mixer, beat the
   cream cheese on a medium-high speed for about 1 minute until smooth.
   Add the cane juice and vanilla extract and mix until combined. Stop and
   scrape down the side of the bowl. Add the egg replacer and beat for
   30 seconds on a medium-high speed.

4. Unwrap one chilled cookie dough round and place it on the base of
   the springform tin. Spoon the cheesecake filling on top. Unwrap and
   place the second cookie dough round on top. Cover the cheesecake with
   foil to prevent the cookie from burning and bake for 40 minutes. Then
   remove the foil and bake for a further 5–10 minutes, until the centre is
   slightly firm. Cool the cheesecake, wrapped in cling film in its tin, in the
   refrigerator for 4–6 hours or overnight.

5. Remove the chilled cheesecake from the refrigerator. Transfer from the
   tin to a serving dish. Slice the cheesecake and dip the round end of each
   slice in tempered chocolate before serving.

VANILLA PUMPKIN CHEESECAKE

 SERVES 8–10

This recipe always reminds me of autumn. The creamy vanilla and pumpkin filling on top of spicy gingernut and pecan nut crust is truly delicious. Decorate with a gingernut biscuit and coconut whipped cream. Vanilla Pumpkin Cheesecake would be a great addition to any special-occasion dessert table.

CRUST

290g crushed gingernut biscuits, plus 8–10 whole for decorating

35g shelled pecan nuts, chopped

85g butter substitute, melted

VANILLA CHEESECAKE FILLING

675g tofu cream cheese, at room temperature

130g evaporated cane juice

1 teaspoon vanilla extract

4½ teaspoons egg replacer, whisked with 6 tablespoons warm water

PUMPKIN CHEESECAKE FILLING

245g canned pumpkin purée

45g evaporated cane juice

2 teaspoons ground cinnamon

1 teaspoon pumpkin pie spice or mixed spice

Coconut Whipped Cream, for decorating (see page 13)

1. Preheat the oven to 150°C/300°F/Gas Mark 2 if using a dark springform tin, or 160°C/325°F/Gas Mark 3 if using a silver springform tin.

2. MAKE THE CRUST. Grind the gingernuts in a food processor until they are finely crushed. Add the pecans and process until just combined. Add the melted butter substitute and mix well. Press firmly onto the base and 4cm up the side of a springform tin.

3. NEXT MAKE THE VANILLA CHEESECAKE FILLING. Using a stand mixer, beat the cream cheese on a medium-high speed for about 20 seconds until smooth. Add the cane juice and mix on a medium speed for about 1 minute until combined. Add the vanilla extract and mix on a high speed for 30 seconds. Stop and scrape down the side of the bowl. Add the egg replacer and beat until just blended. Reserve 300ml of the filling in a medium bowl.

4. MAKE THE PUMPKIN CHEESECAKE FILLING. Combine the reserved 300ml vanilla cheesecake filling, pumpkin purée, cane juice, cinnamon and pumpkin pie spice.

5. Spoon half of the vanilla cheesecake filling into the crust. Top with spoonfuls of the pumpkin filling and vanilla filling in repeating layers. Run a knife through the fillings to create a marbled effect. Bake for 45–50 minutes, until the centre is almost set. Cheesecake should be custard-like in texture, so don't overbake!

6. Run a small knife between the cheesecake and the tin to loosen the cake, making sure to let it cool before removing from the tin. Refrigerate for at least 4 hours; overnight is best. Decorate each slice with a small dollop of Coconut Whipped Cream and a gingernut biscuit.

✳ Cakes of all Kinds ✳

✳ RECIPE LIST ✳

YELLOW CAKE WITH CHOCOLATE SOUR CREAM FROSTING

 SERVES 8–10

I took a classic 'Birthday Cake' of yellow cake and chocolate icing and kicked it up a notch with a rich and fudgy chocolate sour cream frosting. Sprinkle with coloured sugar for an extra-festive look.

225g butter substitute, at room temperature

255g evaporated cane juice

2 teaspoons vanilla extract

390g unbleached plain flour

4 teaspoons baking powder

6 teaspoons egg replacer, whisked with 8 tablespoons warm water

240ml soya milk

1 tablespoon cider vinegar

CHOCOLATE SOUR CREAM FROSTING

360g dairy-free and gluten-free chocolate chips

115g butter substitute

2 teaspoons vanilla extract

¼ teaspoon salt

305g tofu sour cream

980g organic icing sugar

1. Preheat the oven to 180°C/350°F./Gas Mark 4. Grease and flour two 23cm round sandwich tins.

2. Using a stand mixer, beat together the butter substitute, cane juice and vanilla extract on a medium speed for about 20 seconds until combined. Stop and scrape down the side of the bowl, then increase the speed to high and beat the mixture for about 2 minutes until light and fluffy.

3. In a small bowl, mix together the flour and baking powder. In a separate bowl, combine the egg replacer, soya milk and vinegar. Alternate adding the dry and wet ingredients, starting and ending with the dry ingredients, and beat for 10 seconds after each addition. Stop and scrape down the side of the bowl, making sure that all the butter substitute is incorporated. Pour into the 2 prepared cake tins.

4. Bake the cakes for 22–25 minutes, or until a wooden skewer inserted in the centre of a cake comes out clean. Cool in the tins on wire racks for 10 minutes, then flip the tins over to release the cakes. Leave to cool for a further 30 minutes.

5. MEANWHILE, MAKE THE CHOCOLATE SOUR CREAM FROSTING. Melt the chocolate chips and butter substitute for 45 seconds in a microwave-safe bow in the microwavel. Remove from the microwave and stir until the chocolate is completely melted and combined with the butter. Add the vanilla extract, salt and sour cream, stirring until combined. Pour into the mixer and, with the motor running on a medium speed, add the icing sugar 280g at a time until a desired consistency is reached.

6. Place one cooled cake on a serving dish. Using an offset spatula, spread a third of the frosting on top. Add the second cake and spread or pipe the remaining frosting on the top of the cake, and side if you like.

CARROT CAKE

This carrot cake recipe came from my Aunt Maria. The secret ingredients are coconut and pineapple. The coconut lends a rich buttery flavour and the pineapple keeps the carrot cake super-moist.

325g unbleached plain flour

340g evaporated cane juice

2 teaspoons baking powder

1 teaspoon bicarbonate of soda

1 teaspoon salt

2½ teaspoons ground cinnamon

95g dried unsweetened shredded coconut

175g shelled walnuts, chopped

240ml vegetable oil

220g finely grated carrots, plus extra whole carrots for decorating (optional)

80g raisins

225g drained crushed pineapple

1 teaspoon vanilla extract

3 teaspoons egg replacer, whisked with 4 tablespoons warm water

CREAM CHEESE FROSTING

85g butter substitute, at room temperature

225g tofu cream cheese, at room temperature

1 teaspoon vanilla extract

630g organic icing sugar

1. Preheat the oven to 180°C/350°F/Gas Mark 4. Grease and flour two 23cm round sandwich tins.

2. Using a stand mixer, combine the flour, cane juice, baking powder, bicarbonate of soda, salt, cinnamon, coconut and 60g of the walnuts. Add the oil, carrots, raisins, pineapple and vanilla extract. Mix for 30 seconds on a medium speed. Stop and scrape down the side of bowl. Add the egg replacer and mix for a further 30 seconds.

3. Divide the cake mixture between the two prepared baking tins and bake for 30–35 minutes, or until a wooden skewer inserted in the centre of the cakes comes out clean. Cool the tins on wire racks for 10 minutes, then flip the tins over to release the cakes. Leave to cool for a further 45 minutes on the wire racks.

4. MEANWHILE, MAKE THE CREAM CHEESE FROSTING. Using the mixer, beat together the butter substitute, cream cheese and vanilla extract until smooth. Scrape down the side of the bowl and mix on a medium speed for a further 20 seconds. Decrease the speed to low and add the icing sugar 140g at a time, stopping and scraping down the side of the bowl after each addition. Once all the icing sugar is combined, beat for a further 1 minute on a high speed.

5. Place one cooled cake on a serving plate and spread with about a third of the frosting in an even layer. Top with the second cake and spread the remaining cream cheese frosting on the top and side of the cake. Decorate with the remaining walnuts around the side of the cake. For an extra decorative touch, peel long strips of carrot with a vegetable peeler, roll up and position around the edge of the cake. Store in the refrigerator for up to 10 days.

RED VELVET CAKE

SERVES 8–10

I make this moist and delicious cake vegan by using soya milk mixed with cider vinegar to make a 'buttermilk', an essential ingredient in all red velvet cakes.

170g butter substitute

385g evaporated cane juice

1 teaspoon salt

3 tablespoons cocoa powder, sifted

4½ teaspoons egg replacer, whisked with 6 tablespoons warm water

360ml soya milk

2 tablespoons plus 2 teaspoons cider vinegar

2 teaspoons vanilla extract

3 tablespoons natural red food colouring

490g unbleached plain flour

2 teaspoons bicarbonate of soda

Cream Cheese Frosting (page 66)

50g pecan halves, for decorating

1. Preheat the oven to 180°C/350°F/Gas Mark 4. Grease and flour three 23cm round sandwich tins.

2. Using a stand mixer, beat together the butter substitute, cane juice, salt and cocoa powder on a medium speed for about 2 minutes until light and fluffy.

3. In a separate bowl, whisk the egg replacer with the soya milk, the 2 tablespoons vinegar, vanilla extract and red food colouring until well combined. With the stand mixer running, add the wet ingredients, alternating with the flour, to the mixer bowl, stopping and scraping down the side and base of the bowl as needed, until all of the ingredients are well combined.

4. In a small bowl, mix together the bicarbonate of soda and the remaining 2 teaspoons vinegar. Fold into the cake mixture. Divide the mixture between the prepared baking tins and bake immediately for 25–30 minutes, or until a wooden skewer inserted in the centre of a cake comes out clean. Cool in the tins on wire racks for 10 minutes, then flip the tins over to release the cakes. Leave to cool for a further 45 minutes.

5. Sandwich the cakes together with about a third of the Cream Cheese Frosting. Spread the remainder over the top and side of the cake, adding some extra piped frosting if you like. Decorate with the pecan halves.

PUMPKIN SPICE CAKE

This pumpkin spice cake is super-moist and flavourful. It will definitely beat any non-vegan version. A sweet cream cheese frosting complements the spice of cinnamon and pumpkin.

130g unbleached plain flour
130g wholemeal plain flour
240g soft dark brown sugar
2 teaspoons baking powder
1 teaspoon bicarbonate of soda
½ teaspoon salt
2 teaspoons ground cinnamon
¼ teaspoon pumpkin pie spice or mixed spice

120ml vegetable oil
1 teaspoon vanilla extract
425g canned pumpkin purée
120ml soya milk
3 teaspoons egg replacer, whisked with 4 tablespoons warm water

Cream Cheese Frosting (page 66)

1. Preheat the oven to 180°C/350°F/Gas Mark 4. Grease and flour a 23 x 33cm baking tin.
2. Using a stand mixer, combine the flours, brown sugar, baking powder, bicarbonate of soda, salt, cinnamon and pumpkin pie spice. Add the oil, vanilla extract, pumpkin and soya milk and mix on a medium speed for 30 seconds. Stop and scrape down the side of the bowl. Add the egg replacer and mix for another 30 seconds. Spread the cake mixture into the prepared baking tin.
3. Bake for 25–30 minutes, or until a wooden skewer inserted in the centre of the cake comes out clean. Cool in the tin on a wire rack for at least 1 hour. Invert the tin onto a serving platter and spread with the Cream Cheese Frosting.

PUMPKIN CUPCAKES

For this recipe I took my moist yellow cake and added pumpkin purée, pumpkin pie spice and cinnamon for a lightly pumpkin-flavoured cupcake. You can make these in standard-sized cupcake cases or in minis, as shown in the photograph on page 2 of this book. They are delicious for breakfast, served with hot coffee or tea.

115g butter substitute

130g evaporated cane juice

1 teaspoon vanilla extract

195g unbleached plain flour

2 teaspoons baking powder

125g pumpkin purée

½ teaspoon pumpkin pie spice or mixed spice, plus extra for sprinkling

½ teaspoon ground cinnamon

3 teaspoons egg replacer, whisked with 4 tablespoons warm water

120ml soya milk

Cream Cheese Frosting (page 66)

1. Preheat the oven to 180°C/350°F/Gas Mark 4. Line two standard-sized 6-hole muffin tins with paper cases.

2. Using a stand mixer, beat together the butter substitute, cane juice and vanilla extract until light and fluffy. Stop and scrape down the side of the bowl. Add the flour, baking powder, pumpkin, pumpkin pie spice and cinnamon. Mix for 30 seconds on a low speed. Add the egg replacer and soya milk and beat for 30 seconds on a medium speed. Scoop 4 tablespoons of the mixture into each paper case.

3. Bake for 15–18 minutes, or until a wooden skewer inserted in the centre of a cupcake comes out clean. Cool in the tins on wire racks for 30 minutes before removing the cupcakes in their cases. Spread or pipe the cooled cupcakes with the Cream Cheese Frosting, then sprinkle with extra pumpkin pie spice.

RASPBERRY BUTTERCREAM CAKE

SERVES 8–10

Raspberry Buttercream Cake is a moist cake perfect for summer cooking. I love how the raspberries add a burst of flavour and colour to the cake. Serve with raspberry iced tea and mint.

CAKE

225g butter substitute, at room temperature

255g evaporated cane juice

2 teaspoons vanilla extract

390g unbleached plain flour

4 teaspoons baking powder

6 teaspoons egg replacer, whisked with 8 tablespoons warm water

240ml soya milk

1 tablespoon cider vinegar

125g raspberries, plus extra for decorating

BUTTERCREAM

225g butter substitute, at room temperature

420g organic icing sugar

1 teaspoon vanilla extract

2 tablespoons water (optional)

1. Preheat the oven to 180°C/350°F/Gas Mark 4. Grease and flour three 23cm round sandwich tins.

2. FIRST MAKE THE CAKE. Using a stand mixer, beat together the butter substitute, cane juice and vanilla extract on a medium speed until combined. Stop and scrape down the side of the bowl, then turn the mixer to a high speed and beat for about 2 minutes until light and fluffy.

3. Mix together the flour and baking powder in a small bowl. In a separate bowl, mix together the egg replacer, soya milk and vinegar. Alternate adding the dry and wet ingredients to the mixer bowl, starting and ending with the dry ingredients. After each addition, beat for 10 seconds on a low speed, then stop and scrape down the side of the bowl, making sure that all the butter substitute is incorporated.

4. Cut the raspberries into quarters and gently fold into the cake mixture. Pour the mixture into the prepared baking tins.

5. Bake the cakes for 22–25 minutes, or until a wooden skewer inserted in the centre of a cake comes out clean. Cool the tins on wire racks for 10 minutes, then flip the tins over to release the cakes. Leave to cool for a further 30 minutes.

6. MEANWHILE, MAKE THE BUTTERCREAM. Using the mixer, beat the butter substitute until smooth. Stop and scrape down the side and base of the bowl. Add the icing sugar 140g at a time, mixing on a low speed after each addition. Add the vanilla extract and beat for 1 minute on a high speed. If the frosting is too thick to spread, add the water a tablespoon at a time. Beat for a further 2 minutes until light and fluffy.

7. Sandwich the cakes together with a third of the buttercream. Spread the remainder over the top and side of the cake. Decorate with raspberries.

COCONUT CAKE

 SERVES 12–15

Everyone needs a fantastic coconut cake recipe. A beautiful cake with tons of rich buttery coconut flavour, serve it outside on a hot summer day with freshly squeezed lemonade.

225g butter substitute, at room temperature

255g evaporated cane juice

2 teaspoons vanilla extract

95g dried unsweetened shredded coconut

390g unbleached plain flour

4 teaspoons baking powder

6 teaspoons egg replacer, whisked with 8 tablespoons warm water

240ml soya milk

1 tablespoon cider vinegar

COCONUT BUTTERCREAM

225g butter substitute, at room temperature

1 teaspoon vanilla extract

2 tablespoons water

420g organic icing sugar

200g dried unsweetened shredded coconut

1. Preheat the oven to 180°C/350°F/Gas Mark 4. Grease and flour three 23cm round sandwich tins.

2. Using a stand mixer, beat together the butter substitute, cane juice, vanilla extract and coconut on a medium speed until combined. Stop and scrape down the side of the bowl, then increase the speed to high and beat the mixture for about 2 minutes until light and fluffy.

3. Mix together the flour and baking powder in a small bowl. In a separate bowl, combine the egg replacer, soya milk and vinegar. Alternate adding the dry and wet ingredients to the mixer bowl, starting and ending with the dry ingredients. After each addition, beat on a low speed for 10 seconds. Stop and scrape down the side of the bowl, making sure that all the butter substitute is incorporated. Pour into the prepared baking tins.

4. Bake for 20–25 minutes, or until a wooden skewer inserted in the centre of a cake comes out clean. Cool in the tins on wire racks for 10 minutes, then flip the tins over to release the cakes. Cool for a further 45 minutes.

5. MEANWHILE, MAKE THE COCONUT BUTTERCREAM. Using the mixer, beat the butter substitute on a medium speed for about 20 seconds until smooth. Stop and scrape down the side of the bowl. Add the vanilla extract, water and icing sugar and mix for 30 seconds on a low speed until combined, then beat for a further 2 minutes on a high speed until light and fluffy. Fold in 50g of the coconut.

6. Place one of the cooled cakes on a serving dish. Spread with about 115g of the buttercream and top with 25g of the coconut. Add the second cake and repeat. Add the third layer and spread the remaining buttercream on the top and side of the cake. With your hand, press the remaining coconut to the side and top of the cake.

PINEAPPLE UPSIDE-DOWN CAKE

Pineapple upside-down cake is one of my dad's favourite recipes. When you take the cake out of the oven and flip it over, the gooey brown sugar–pineapple topping drips down the side of the moist yellow cake for a truly decadent experience. This is delicious served with your choice of non-dairy ice cream.

115g butter substitute

170g evaporated cane juice

195g unbleached plain flour

2 teaspoons baking powder

½ teaspoon salt

¼ teaspoon cream of tartar

1 teaspoon vanilla extract

120ml soya milk

3 teaspoons egg replacer, whisked with 4 tablespoons warm water

BROWN SUGAR PINEAPPLE TOPPING

55g butter substitute, melted

120g soft dark brown sugar

550g canned pineapple rings, drained

1. Preheat the oven to 180°C/350°F/Gas Mark 4. Line the base of a 23cm round cake tin with greased parchment paper.

2. Using a stand mixer, beat together the butter substitute and cane juice for about 2 minutes until light and fluffy. Stop and scrape down the side of the bowl. Add the flour, baking powder, salt and cream of tartar. Mix for 30 seconds on a medium speed. Add the vanilla extract, soya milk and egg replacer and mix until combined. Set aside.

3. MAKE THE TOPPING. In a small bowl, combine the butter substitute and brown sugar. Spread it into the prepared cake tin. Arrange the pineapple rings over the brown sugar mixture in one layer. Pour the cake mixture on top and smooth with a spatula.

4. Bake the cake for 40–50 minutes, or until a wooden skewer inserted in the centre of the cake comes out clean. Cool the tin on a wire rack for 10 minutes, then invert the tin onto a serving dish to release the cake. Leave to cool for a further 45 minutes before serving.

LEMON BUTTERCREAM CAKE

 SERVES 12–15

This refreshing cake has a great flavour combination of sweet and tart lemons with rich buttery coconut flakes. Garnish it with sliced lemons and lemon zest, and share this new recipe with friends.

225g butter substitute, at room temperature

255g evaporated cane juice

2 teaspoons vanilla extract

390g unbleached plain flour

4 teaspoons baking powder

6 teaspoons egg replacer, whisked with 8 tablespoons warm water

240ml soya milk

1 tablespoon cider vinegar

1 teaspoon lemon extract

LEMON BUTTERCREAM

225g butter substitute, at room temperature

3 tablespoons fresh lemon juice

1 teaspoon vanilla extract

420g organic icing sugar

TOPPING

200g dried unsweetened shredded coconut

1 teaspoon grated lemon zest

l lemon, thinly cut into 8 slices

1. Preheat the oven to 180°C/350°F/Gas Mark 4. Grease and flour two 23cm round sandwich tins.

2. Using a stand mixer, beat together the butter substitute, cane juice and vanilla extract on a medium speed for about 30 seconds until combined. Stop and scrape down the side of the bowl, then increase the speed to high and beat the mixture for about 5 minutes until light and fluffy.

3. In a small bowl, mix together the flour and baking powder. In a separate bowl, combine the egg replacer, soya milk, vinegar and lemon extract. Alternate adding the dry and wet ingredients to the mixer bowl, starting and ending with the dry ingredients, and beating for 10 seconds after each addition. Stop and scrape down the side of the bowl, making sure that all the butter substitute is incorporated. Pour into the prepared tins.

4. Bake for 20–25 minutes, or until a wooden skewer inserted in the centre of a cake comes out clean. Cool in the tins on a wire rack for 10 minutes, then flip the tins over to release the cakes. Cool for a further 45 minutes.

5. MEANWHILE, MAKE THE LEMON BUTTERCREAM. Using the mixer, beat the butter substitute on a medium speed for about 20 seconds until smooth. Add the lemon juice and mix for 30 seconds. Stop and scrape down the side of the bowl. Add the vanilla extract and icing sugar and mix for 30 seconds on a low speed until well combined, then beat for a further 2 minutes on a high speed until light and fluffy.

6. Place one cooled cake on a serving dish. Using an offset spatula, spread with about a third of the lemon buttercream and top with 50g of the coconut. Add the second cake and spread the remaining buttercream on the top and side of the cake. Press the remaining coconut to the side of the cake with your hand. Decorate with the lemon zest and lemon slices.

LEMON BUTTERCREAM CUPCAKES

 MAKES 12–15

A derivative of the Lemon Buttercream Cake, these moist and flavourful cupcakes are great for a picnic, party or just a treat after work. The slightly tart buttercream gives a burst of flavour to the sweet lemony cupcake. Sprinkle the lemon zest on top for a pleasing pop of colour.

225g butter substitute, at room temperature

255g evaporated cane juice

2 teaspoons vanilla extract

3 teaspoons lemon extract

1 tablespoon grated lemon zest, plus extra for decorating

390g unbleached plain flour

4 teaspoons baking powder

6 teaspoons egg replacer, whisked with 8 tablespoons warm water

240ml soya milk

1 tablespoon cider vinegar

Lemon Buttercream (page 77)

1. Preheat the oven to 180°C/350°F/Gas Mark 4. Line 15 standard-sized holes of two cupcake tins with paper cases.

2. Using a stand mixer, beat together the butter substitute, cane juice, vanilla extract, lemon extract and lemon zest until combined. Stop and scrape down the side and base of the bowl. Increase the speed to high and beat the mixture for about 2 minutes until light and fluffy.

3. In a medium bowl, mix together the flour and baking powder. In a separate bowl, combine the egg replacer, soya milk and vinegar. Alternate adding the dry and wet ingredients to the mixer bowl, starting and ending with the dry ingredients, and beat for 10 seconds after each addition. Stop and scrape down the side of the bowl, making sure that all the butter substitute is incorporated. Beat for a further 30 seconds on a medium speed. Spoon the mixture into the paper cases until a quarter of the way up.

4. Bake for 20–25 minutes, or until a wooden skewer inserted in the centre of a cupcake comes out clean. Cool in the tins on wire racks for 10 minutes, then remove the cupcakes in their cases and leave to cool for a further 20 minutes. Spread or pipe the top of each cupcake with the lemon buttercream and decorate with lemon zest.

✳ *Gluten-Free* ✳ CRANBERRY ORANGE BUNDT CAKE

 SERVES 10–12

> Moist and gluten-free are not usually in the same sentence, but this bundt cake is very moist indeed. The unique flavour combinations of cranberry and pumpkin spice mixed with pecan and orange add a depth of taste unlike anything you have tried before. And it's so delicious when drizzled with an orange juice–sugar glaze.

365g Gluten-Free Flour Mix (page 13)

1 teaspoon baking powder

½ teaspoon bicarbonate of soda

1 teaspoon salt

1 tablespoon pumpkin pie spice or mixed spice

115g butter substitute

85g evaporated cane juice

¼ teaspoon grated orange zest

365g unsweetened apple sauce or apple purée

3 teaspoons egg replacer, whisked with 4 tablespoons warm water

60g shelled pecan nuts, chopped

120g organic dried cranberries

ORANGE GLAZE

140g organic icing sugar

2 tablespoons orange juice

1. Preheat the oven to 180°C/350°F/Gas Mark 4. Grease and flour a bundt cake tin.

2. In a large bowl, combine the flour, baking powder, bicarbonate of soda, salt and pumpkin pie spice. Set aside.

3. Using a stand mixer, beat together the butter substitute, cane juice and orange zest on a high speed for about 2 minutes until light and fluffy. Stop and scrape down the side of the bowl. Add the apple sauce, flour mixture, egg replacer, pecans and cranberries and mix for 30 seconds on a high speed. Pour the cake mixture into the prepared bundt tin.

4. Bake the cake for 50–60 minutes, or until a wooden skewer inserted in the centre comes out clean. Cool in the tin on a wire rack for 10 minutes, then invert the tin to release the cake. Leave to cool for 1 hour.

5. Meanwhile, in a small bowl, beat together the icing sugar and orange juice until combined. Pour over the cooled cake before serving.

CHOCOLATE GANACHE CAKE

 SERVES 8–10

My stepmum learned this recipe from her mum, and passed it on to me when I was in middle school. The coffee brings out the rich chocolate flavour. One of my all-time bestsellers.

CHOCOLATE CAKE

230g unbleached plain flour
340g evaporated cane juice
75g cocoa powder, sifted
1 teaspoon baking powder
2 teaspoons bicarbonate of soda
1 teaspoon salt
240ml strong coffee, cooled
120ml vegetable oil
1 teaspoon vanilla extract
240ml soya milk and cider vinegar*
3 teaspoons egg replacer, whisked with 4 tablespoons warm water

CHOCOLATE BUTTERCREAM

225g butter substitute, softened
420g organic icing sugar
25g cocoa powder, sifted
2 tablespoons water

CHOCOLATE GANACHE

180g dairy-free and gluten-free chocolate chips
85g butter substitute

*Pour 1 tablespoon cider vinegar into a measuring jug, then add the soya milk to equal 240ml

1. Preheat the oven to 180°C/350°F/Gas Mark 4. Grease and flour two 23cm round sandwich tins.

2. In a stand mixer, place the flour, cane juice, cocoa powder, baking powder, bicarbonate of soda and salt and stir to combine.

3. In a separate bowl, whisk together the cooled coffee, oil, vanilla extract and soya milk/vinegar mixture. Turn the mixer to a low speed and slowly pour the liquid mixture into the dry ingredients. Mix for 1 minute. Stop and scrape down the side and base of the bowl. Add the egg replacer and mix again for 1 minute on a medium speed. The cake mixture will be very thin. Divide it between the prepared cake tins.

4. Bake for 25–30 minutes, or until a wooden skewer inserted in the centre of a cake comes out clean. Cool in the tins on wire racks for 10 minutes, then flip the tins over to release the cakes. Leave to cool for 1 hour.

5. MEANWHILE, MAKE THE CHOCOLATE BUTTERCREAM. Using the mixer, beat the butter substitute on a medium speed for about 20 seconds until smooth in texture. Stop and scrape down the side of the bowl. Add the icing sugar and cocoa powder and mix for 1 minute on a low speed. Add the water and mix on a medium speed until combined, then increase the speed to high and beat for a further 2 minutes until the buttercream is light and fluffy. Set aside.

6. MAKE THE CHOCOLATE GANACHE. In a microwave-safe bowl, melt the chocolate chips and butter substitute in the microwave on 75% power for 45 seconds. Remove from the microwave and stir until the chocolate is completely melted. Set aside.

7. Place one cooled cake on a serving plate. Spread about a third of the chocolate buttercream on top. Place the second cake on top and spread the remaining buttercream on the top and side of the cake. Pour the ganache on top of the frosted cake and spread it over the side of the cake with an offset spatula.

GERMAN CHOCOLATE CAKE

 SERVES 8–10

The homemade caramel, coconut and pecan frosting in this recipe is to die for. Be careful if you make this with company – you may not get the frosting onto the cake before it's polished off in the bowl! I guarantee that everyone will want your recipe and no one will be able to tell it's vegan.

230g unbleached plain flour

340g evaporated cane juice

75g cocoa powder, sifted

1 teaspoon baking powder

2 teaspoons bicarbonate of soda

1 teaspoon salt

240ml strong coffee, cooled

120ml vegetable oil

1 teaspoon vanilla extract

240ml soya milk and cider vinegar*

3 teaspoons egg replacer, whisked with 4 tablespoons warm water

GERMAN CHOCOLATE FROSTING

115g butter substitute

120ml soya milk

140g dried unsweetened shredded coconut

115g shelled pecan nuts, chopped, plus extra for decorating (optional)

85g evaporated cane juice

1 teaspoon vanilla extract

Chocolate Buttercream (page 82)

*Pour 1 tablespoon cider vinegar into a measuring jug, then add the soya milk to equal 240ml.

1. Preheat the oven to 180°C/350°F/Gas Mark 4. Grease and flour two 23cm round sandwich tins.

2. In a stand mixer, combine the flour, cane juice, cocoa powder, baking powder, bicarbonate of soda and salt. Stir to combine.

3. In a separate bowl, whisk together the cooled coffee, oil, vanilla extract and soya milk/vinegar mixture. Turn the mixer onto a low speed and slowly pour the liquid mixture into the dry ingredients. Mix for 1 minute. Stop and scrape down the side and base of the bowl. Add the egg replacer and mix again for 1 minute. The cake mixture will be very thin. Divide it between the prepared cake tins.

4. Bake for 25–30 minutes, or until a wooden skewer inserted in the centre of a cake comes out clean. Cool in the tins on wire racks for 10 minutes, then flip the tins over to release the cakes. Leave to cool for 1 hour.

5. MEANWHILE, MAKE THE GERMAN CHOCOLATE FROSTING. In a saucepan, melt the butter substitute. Add the soya milk, coconut, pecans, cane juice and vanilla extract. Stir until combined, then heat for 2 minutes or until the mixture comes to the boil.

6. Place one cooled cake on a serving plate. Using an offset spatula, spread half of the German Chocolate Frosting on top, then add the second cake and spread the remaining frosting on top of that. Frost the side of the cake with the Chocolate Buttercream. If you like, decorate the top of the cake with piped Chocolate Buttercream and press some extra chopped pecans into the base of the cake side.

✳ *Gluten-Free* ✳
CHOCOLATE CUPCAKES

 MAKES 24

Here I took my famous chocolate cake recipe and used my gluten-free flour mix in place of plain flour. Moist and delicious as ever, you will not be able to tell that these cupcakes are gluten-free.

255g Gluten Free Flour Mix (page 13)

340g evaporated cane juice

75g cocoa powder, sifted

1 teaspoon baking powder

2 teaspoons bicarbonate of soda

1 teaspoon salt

240ml strong coffee, cooled

120ml vegetable oil

1 teaspoon vanilla extract

240ml soya milk and cider vinegar*

3 teaspoons egg replacer, whisked with 4 tablespoons warm water

COCONUT BUTTERCREAM

225g butter substitute, at room temperature

420g organic icing sugar

140g dried unsweetened shredded coconut

2 tablespoons water

1 teaspoon vanilla extract

Chocolate Buttercream (page 82)

*Pour 1 tablespoon cider vinegar into a measuring jug, and add soya milk to equal 240ml.

1. Preheat the oven to 180°C/350°F/Gas Mark 4. Line the holes of two standard-sized 12-hole cupcake tins with paper cases.

2. In a stand mixer, combine the flour, cane juice, cocoa powder, baking powder, bicarbonate of soda and salt. In a separate bowl, whisk together the cooled coffee, oil, vanilla extract and soya milk/vinegar mixture. Turn the mixer onto a medium speed and slowly pour the liquid mixture into the dry ingredients. Mix for 1 minute. Add the egg replacer and mix again for 1 minute. The cake mixture will be thin. Scoop 4 tablespoons of the mixture into each paper case.

3. Bake for 18–20 minutes, or until a wooden skewer inserted in the centre of a cupcake comes out clean. Cool on wire racks for 30 minutes.

4. MEANWHILE, MAKE THE COCONUT BUTTERCREAM. Using the mixer, beat the butter substitute until smooth in texture. Stop and scrape down the side of the bowl. Add the icing sugar and mix for 1 minute on a low speed. Add half of the coconut, the water and vanilla extract. Mix on a high speed for 30 seconds until combined and fluffy.

5. Frost half of the cooled cupcakes with the Coconut Buttercream and top with the remaining coconut. Frost the other half of the cooled cupcakes with the Chocolate Buttercream.

BLACK BOTTOMS

MAKES 14

Black Bottoms are a classic dessert that my relatives always had at family gatherings. They are a real crowd pleaser, and with these vegan and gluten-free variations, now everyone can enjoy these fun-looking sweet cupcakes.

CHOCOLATE CAKE

195g unbleached plain flour or 220g Gluten-Free Flour Mix (page 13)

170g evaporated cane juice

1 teaspoon bicarbonate of soda

25g cocoa powder, sifted

240ml water

80ml vegetable oil

1 teaspoon vanilla extract

1 tablespoon cider vinegar

CREAM CHEESE TOPPING

225g tofu cream cheese, at room temperature

60g evaporated cane juice

¼ teaspoon salt

1½ teaspoons egg replacer, whisked with 1 tablespoon warm water

180g dairy-free and gluten-free chocolate chips

1. Preheat the oven to 180°C/350°F/Gas Mark 4. Line 14 holes of two standard-sized muffin tins with paper cases.

2. MAKE THE CHOCOLATE CAKE. In a medium bowl, mix together the flour, cane juice, bicarbonate of soda and cocoa powder. Pour in the water, oil, vanilla extract and vinegar. Stir until combined. Scoop 4 tablespoons of the mixture into each paper case. Set aside.

3. NEXT MAKE THE CREAM CHEESE TOPPING. Using a stand mixer, beat the cream cheese until smooth. Add the cane juice and salt and mix for 30 seconds, then stop and scrape down the side of the bowl. Add the egg replacer and blend on a medium speed for 30 seconds. Stir in the chocolate chips. Spoon 2 tablespoons of the mixture on top of each chocolate bottom.

4. Bake the black bottoms for 18–22 minutes, or until a wooden skewer inserted in the centre of a cupcake comes out clean. Cool on wire racks. Store the cupcakes in the refrigerator for up to 14 days. These can also be frozen for up to 3 months in an airtight container.

PB&J CUPCAKES

 MAKES 18

PB&J was my favourite sandwich growing up, so I decided to make it into a cupcake. Yellow cake is used for the two slices of bread, strawberry jam is sandwiched in between and a rich peanut butter buttercream ties it all together. If only I could have had these in my lunchbox when I was at school!

225g butter substitute

255g evaporated cane juice

2 teaspoons vanilla extract

390g unbleached plain flour

4 teaspoons baking powder

6 teaspoons egg replacer, whisked with 8 tablespoons warm water

240ml soya milk

PEANUT BUTTER BUTTERCREAM

225g butter substitute, softened

130g unsweetened peanut butter

420g organic icing sugar

1 tablespoon soya milk

1 teaspoon vanilla extract

350g strawberry jam, for filling

1. Preheat the oven to 180°C/350°F/Gas Mark 4. Line 18 holes of two standard-sized muffin tins with paper cases.

2. Using a stand mixer, beat together the butter substitute, cane juice and vanilla extract on a medium speed for about 3 minutes until light and fluffy. Stop and scrape down the side of the bowl.

3. Sift the flour and baking powder together into a small bowl. Set aside. In a separate bowl, combine the egg replacer and soya milk. With the motor running on a low speed, alternate adding the dry and wet ingredients to the mixer bowl, beginning and ending with the dry ingredients. Beat for 30 seconds on a medium speed. Stop and scrape down the side and base of the bowl, then mix for a further 30 seconds. Scoop 4 tablespoons of the mixture into each paper case.

4. Bake the cupcakes for 18–20 minutes, or until a wooden skewer inserted in the centre of a cupcake comes out clean. Cool in the tins on wire racks for about 30 minutes before removing the cupcakes.

5. MEANWHILE, MAKE THE PEANUT BUTTER BUTTERCREAM. Using the mixer, beat the butter substitute on a medium speed for about 30 seconds until smooth. Stop and scrape down the side of the bowl. Add the peanut butter and mix for 30 seconds. Add the icing sugar, soya milk and vanilla extract and mix on a low speed until the sugar is incorporated, then mix on a high speed for 1 minute until fluffy.

6. When the cupcakes are cool, unwrap each cupcake and cut it in half. Spoon 1 tablespoon strawberry jam onto the bottom half of each cupcake. Spread or pipe the top half of each cupcake with the Peanut Butter Buttercream, then sandwich the two halves together, with the jam on the bottom.

STRAWBERRY LEMON CUPCAKES

 MAKES 20

A fun recipe to make with your family, the strawberry buttercream bursts from these cupcakes and the lemon glaze drips down the sides. Definitely have plenty of napkins on hand when serving.

225g butter substitute, at room temperature

255g evaporated cane juice

2 teaspoons vanilla extract

390g unbleached plain flour

4 teaspoons baking powder

6 teaspoons egg replacer, whisked with 8 tablespoons warm water

240ml soya milk

1 tablespoon cider vinegar

STRAWBERRY BUTTERCREAM

225g butter substitute, at room temperature

45g hulled strawberries

490g organic icing sugar

LEMON GLAZE

140g icing sugar

1 tablespoon lemon juice

1 tablespoon water

1. Preheat the oven to 180°C/350°F/Gas Mark 4. Fill 20 holes of two standard-sized cupcake tins with paper cases.

2. Using a stand mixer, beat together the butter substitute, cane juice and vanilla extract on a medium speed for about 20 seconds until combined. Stop and scrape down the side of the bowl, then increase the speed to high and beat the mixture for about 2 minutes until light and fluffy.

3. In a small bowl, mix together the flour and baking powder. In a separate bowl, combine the egg replacer, soya milk and vinegar. Alternate adding the dry and wet ingredients to the mixer bowl, starting and ending with the dry ingredients, beating for 10 seconds after each addition. Stop and scrape down the side of the bowl, making sure that all the butter substitute is incorporated. Scoop 4 tablespoons of the mixture into each paper case.

4. Bake for 20–25 minutes, or until a wooden skewer inserted in the centre of a cupcake comes out clean. Remove the cupcakes from the tins in their cases and cool on wire racks for 30 minutes.

5. MEANWHILE, MAKE THE STRAWBERRY BUTTERCREAM. Using the mixer, beat the butter substitute on a medium speed for about 30 seconds until smooth. Purée the strawberries in a food processor or blender. Add to the mixer bowl and mix for 30 seconds. Stop and scrape down the side of the bowl. Add the icing sugar and mix for 30 seconds on a low speed until it is incorporated. Beat the buttercream on a high speed for a further 2 minutes until light and fluffy. Set aside.

6. MAKE THE LEMON GLAZE. In a small bowl, beat together the icing sugar, lemon juice and water. Set aside.

7. When the cupcakes are cool, spoon the Strawberry Buttercream into a piping bag or zip-top bag, with the bottom corner cut. Squeeze the buttercream into the top of each cupcake until the cupcake starts to split open. Drizzle with the lemon glaze.

✸ Cookies, Brownies ✸ and Bars

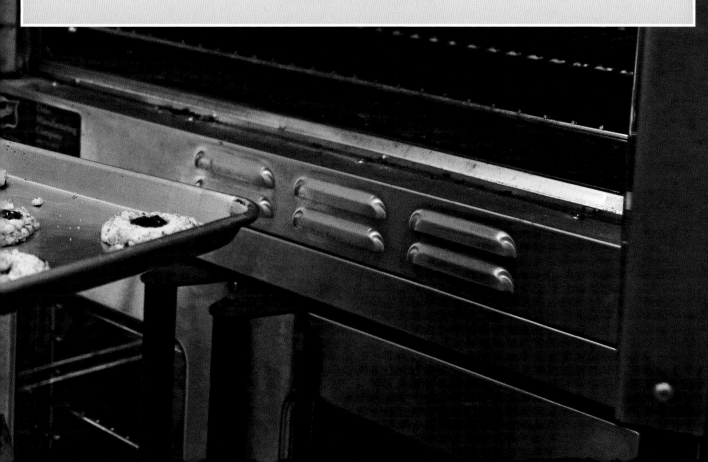

✳ RECIPE LIST ✳

✳ *Gluten-Free* ✳
ALMOND JAM COOKIES

MAKES 9–12

These delicious gluten-free cookies have a nutty almond flavour combined with sweet strawberry jam. An old family recipe, these are great with a glass of peach iced tea.

115g butter substitute

45g evaporated cane juice

1 teaspoon vanilla extract

¼ teaspoon almond extract

145g Gluten-Free Flour Mix (page 13)

¼ teaspoon salt

1½ teaspoons egg replacer, whisked with 2 tablespoons warm water

45g finely chopped almonds

170g organic strawberry jam

1. Preheat the oven to 180°C/350°F/Gas Mark 4. Line two baking sheets with foil or parchment paper.

2. Using a stand mixer, cream the butter substitute and cane juice until light and fluffy. Add the vanilla and almond extracts, mixing until combined. Stop the machine and scrape down the side and base of the bowl. Then add the flour and salt. Mix on a medium speed for 30 seconds. Stop and scrape down the side of the bowl again. Add the egg replacer and mix for 30 seconds until a ball of dough forms. Wrap the cookie dough in cling film and refrigerate for 1 hour.

3. Once the dough is chilled, roll it into 2.5cm balls, flouring your hands as necessary. Spread the chopped almonds on a baking sheet, then roll the balls through them to cover on all sides. Press your thumb into the centre of each ball, fill with ½ teaspoon jam and place on the prepared baking sheets.

4. Bake the cookies for 12–14 minutes, or until they have browned. Place on wire racks to cool. Store in an airtight container.

ALMOND SNICKERDOODLES

This recipe gives the classic Christmas-time cinnamon sugar snickerdoodle cookie a twist with pure almond extract. The almond adds another level of unexpected flavour. These are best served warm right out the oven.

225g butter substitute

255g evaporated cane juice, plus 2 tablespoons for coating

390g unbleached plain flour

1 teaspoon bicarbonate of soda

½ teaspoon salt

1 teaspoon cream of tartar

3 teaspoons egg replacer, whisked with 4 tablespoons warm water

1 teaspoon vanilla extract

1 teaspoon almond extract

2 teaspoons ground cinnamon

1. Preheat the oven to 200°C/400°F/Gas Mark 6. Line two baking sheets with foil or parchment paper.

2. Using a stand mixer, beat together the butter substitute and the 255g cane juice on a medium speed for about 2 minutes until light and fluffy. Stop the machine and scrape down the side of the bowl. Add the flour, bicarbonate of soda, salt and cream of tartar and mix on a medium speed for 1 minute. Stop and scrape down the side of the bowl again. Add the egg replacer and vanilla and almond extracts, then beat on a medium speed for about 30 seconds until a ball of dough forms.

3. Remove the dough from the mixer bowl and roll into 2.5cm balls, flouring your hands as necessary.

4. In a small bowl, combine the remaining 2 tablespoons cane juice with the cinnamon. Roll the cookie dough balls in the mixture to cover all over, then lightly press the tines of a fork into the cookies.

5. Bake the cookies on the prepared baking sheets for 8–10 minutes, or until golden brown. Store in an airtight container for up to a week.

PECAN SHORTBREAD COOKIES

 MAKES 24

Known by many names, such as Mexican Wedding Cookies, Russian Tea Cookies or Snowman Cookies, these treats are loved by all. This vegan version doesn't miss a step. Just delicious.

225g butter substitute

170g evaporated cane juice

260g unbleached plain flour

¼ teaspoon salt

175g shelled pecan nuts, finely chopped

2 teaspoons vanilla extract

70g organic icing sugar

1. Preheat the oven to 180°C/350°F/Gas Mark 4. Line two baking sheets with foil or parchment paper.

2. Using a stand mixer, beat together the butter substitute and cane juice on a high speed for about 2 minutes until light and fluffy. Stop and scrape down the side of the bowl. Add the flour, salt, pecans and vanilla extract and mix for 30 seconds until a ball of dough forms. If the dough is too soft to roll, cover with cling film and refrigerate for 1 hour.

3. Roll the dough into 2.5cm balls, flouring your hands as necessary, and place on the prepared baking sheets.

4. Bake the cookies for 10–12 minutes. Cool on wire racks. Once cooled, roll in the icing sugar. Store in an airtight container at room temperature, or freeze in a freezer bag for up to 3 months.

CHOCOLATE DIGESTIVE BISCUITS

Delicious on their own but also great when making pie crusts, these digestive biscuits have all-natural ingredients and don't have the high-fructose corn syrup like shop-bought brands.

65g unbleached plain flour

195g wholemeal plain flour

85g evaporated cane juice

50g cocoa powder, sifted

½ teaspoon salt

1 teaspoon baking powder

55g butter substitute

2 tablespoons light agave nectar

1 tablespoon molasses or black treacle

300ml water

1. Preheat the oven to 180°C/350°F/Gas Mark 4. Line two baking sheets with foil or parchment paper.

2. Using a stand mixer, combine the flours, half of the cane juice, the cocoa powder, salt and baking powder. With the motor running on a medium speed, add the butter substitute 1 tablespoon at a time, waiting 10 seconds after each addition. Continue mixing for about 1 minute until the mixture resembles coarse sand.

3. Add the agave nectar, molasses and 60ml of the water to the flour mixture and mix on a low speed. Continue adding water, 60ml at a time, until the mixture forms a ball of dough. Wrap in cling film and chill for 1 hour in the refrigerator.

4. Lightly flour your work surface, rolling pin and the ball of chilled dough. Roll the dough out as thinly as possible. Using a knife, cut the dough into squares, or use any shaped biscuit cutter. Place the biscuits on the prepared baking sheets about 2.5cm apart. Prick with a fork, lightly brush with water and sprinkle with the remaining cane juice.

5. Bake for 13–15 minutes, until the crackers are crisp. Store in an airtight container for up to 2 weeks.

AGAVE DIGESTIVE BISCUIT

 MAKES 30

Agave gives this vegan version of a honey digestive biscuit the sweet flavour that honey does without actually using honey. This biscuit is a staple for recipes like s'mores, as seen on the next page.

65g unbleached plain flour

260g wholemeal plain flour

85g evaporated cane juice

½ teaspoon salt

1 teaspoon baking powder

1 teaspoon ground cinnamon

55g butter substitute

2 tablespoons light agave nectar

1 tablespoon molasses or black treacle

300ml water

1. Preheat the oven to 180°C/350°F/Gas Mark 4. Line two baking sheets with foil or parchment paper.

2. Using a stand mixer, combine the flours, half of the cane juice, salt, baking powder and cinnamon. With the motor running on a medium speed, add the butter substitute 1 tablespoon at a time, waiting 10 seconds after each addition. Continue mixing for about 1 minute until the mixture resembles coarse sand.

3. Add the agave nectar, molasses and 60ml of the water to the flour mixture and mix on a low speed. Continue adding water, 60ml at a time, until the mixture forms a ball of dough. Wrap in cling film and chill for 1 hour in the refrigerator.

4. Lightly flour your work surface, a rolling pin and the ball of chilled dough. Roll the dough out as thinly as possible. Using a knife, cut the dough into squares, or use any shaped biscuit cutter. Place the biscuits on the prepared baking sheets about 2.5cm apart. Prick with a fork, lightly brush with water and sprinkle with the remaining cane juice.

5. Bake for 13–15 minutes, until the biscuits are crisp. Store in an airtight container for up to 2 weeks.

S'MORES

S'mores are an all-American summer favourite, traditionally toasted over a campfire. The vegan marshmallows toast just like non-vegan marshmallows and taste a lot better too.

16 Agave Digestive Biscuits
(see opposite)
16 vegan vanilla marshmallows
180g dairy-free and gluten-free
chocolate chips

1. Preheat the oven to 190°C/375°F/Gas Mark 5. Line a baking sheet with foil.
2. Place 8 digestive biscuits onto the prepared baking sheet. Top each biscuit with 2 marshmallows. Heat in the oven for 8 minutes, or until the marshmallows begin to brown and fluff.
3. Meanwhile, in a microwave-safe bowl, melt the chocolate chips in the microwave on 75% power for 2 minutes, stirring after each 30-second interval. Remove from the microwave and stir the chocolate until it is completely melted.
4. Spoon the melted chocolate onto the remaining 8 digestive biscuits. Sandwich the marshmallow-topped biscuits and chocolate-covered biscuits together. Serve immediately.

✳ *Raw* ✳
CINNAMON RAISIN COOKIES

 MAKES 16

This very easy raw recipe – what makes it 'raw' is that nothing is processed or cooked over 29°C/85°F – calls for only 5 ingredients and is super-quick to make. Great for a snack on the go, the walnuts give you a protein kick and the raisins are high in fibre and many essential vitamins.

100g raw shelled walnuts

330g raisins

165g dried unsweetened shredded coconut

1 teaspoon ground cinnamon

2 teaspoons coconut oil

1. Using a food processor, process the walnuts until finely ground. Pour into a bowl.

2. Process the raisins in the food processor for 4 minutes on a high speed until they turn into a paste, stopping and scraping down the side of the bowl as necessary. Add the ground walnuts, 115g of the coconut, the cinnamon and coconut oil. Process on a high speed for 3 minutes, or until all the ingredients come together.

3. Form into sixteen 6cm cookies and press the remaining coconut on both sides of the cookies. Store in the refrigerator for up to 3 days.

PEANUT BUTTER BROWNIES

 MAKES 12–15

The vegan brownie seems to be one of the hardest to master as most come out too cake-like. But my recipe comes out moist and chewy. Adding peanut butter and a chocolate drizzle make these brownies an indulgent treat. These are great for a picnic or barbecue, or served with a glass of your favourite non-dairy milk.

260g unbleached plain flour

340g evaporated cane juice

75g cocoa powder, sifted

1 teaspoon baking powder

1 teaspoon salt

240ml water

240ml vegetable oil

1½ teaspoons vanilla extract

65g natural unsweetened peanut butter

90g dairy-free and gluten-free chocolate chips, melted

1. Preheat the oven to 180°C/350°F/Gas Mark 4. Line and grease a 23 x 33cm baking tin with foil or parchment paper.

2. Using a stand mixer, combine the flour, cane juice, cocoa powder, baking powder and salt. Add the water, oil and vanilla extract and mix on a medium speed for 1 minute until combined. Pour into the prepared baking tin.

3. Spoon the peanut butter onto each corner and the centre of the brownie mixture. Using a table knife, swirl the peanut butter into the brownie mixture to create a marbled effect.

4. Bake for 20–25 minutes. Cool the tin on a wire rack for 30 minutes, then invert the tin on a chopping board and peel away the foil or parchment. Cut into brownies and drizzle with the melted chocolate.

CRÈME DE MENTHE BROWNIES

These brownies were one of my favourite desserts when I was a kid. My Aunt Trisha made them for special occasions and I would anxiously wait for dinner to be over so I could indulge. The moist brownie, cool mint filling and chocolate ganache topping are one of the most delicious combinations you will ever taste.

BROWNIE

260g unbleached plain flour

340g evaporated cane juice

75g cocoa powder, sifted

1 teaspoon baking powder

1 teaspoon salt

240ml water

240ml vegetable oil

1½ teaspoons vanilla extract

CRÈME DE MENTHE FILLING

115g butter substitute, at room temperature

280g organic icing sugar

4 tablespoons Crème de Menthe liqueur

CHOCOLATE GANACHE

180g dairy-free and gluten-free chocolate chips

85g butter substitute

1. Preheat the oven to 180°C/350°F./Gas Mark 4 Grease and lightly flour a 23 x 33cm baking tin.
2. FIRST MAKE THE BROWNIES. Using a stand mixer, combine the flour, cane juice, cocoa powder, baking powder and salt. Add the water, vegetable oil and vanilla extract and mix on a medium speed for 1 minute, or until well combined. Pour into the prepared baking tin. Bake for 20–25 minutes, then cool in the tin on a wire rack for 1 hour.
3. MEANWHILE, MAKE CRÈME DE MENTHE FILLING. Using the mixer, beat the butter substitute until smooth. Stop and scrape down the side of the bowl. Add the icing sugar and liqueur and mix for 1 minute. Spread evenly over the cooled brownie cake.
4. To make the Chocolate Ganache, melt the chocolate chips and butter substitute in a microwave-safe bowl in the microwave for 1 minute. Stir until completely melted and pour over the crème de menthe filling. Spread evenly with an offset spatula. Cover with cling film and place in the freezer immediately for about 10 minutes until set.
5. Cut the chilled mixture into brownies with a sharp knife*. Store in an airtight container in the refrigerator for up to 14 days, or in the freezer for up to 3 months.

*For easier cutting, warm the knife under hot water, dry it and cut the brownies. This will also allow the brownies to have clean edges.

MARSHMALLOW BARS

These easy rice cereal bars are a real throwback to childhood and therefore a comfort treat, but here they feature a quality organic version of the cereal and vegan marshmallows. These bars are also really good dipped in chocolate or peanut butter. Yum!

40g butter substitute
380g vegan marshmallows
180g organic rice cereal

1. In a large saucepan, melt the butter substitute over a medium heat. Once melted, add the marshmallows and heat for about 5 minutes, stirring, until completely melted. Turn the heat off and stir in the cereal.

2. Line the bottom of a 23 x 33cm baking tin with parchment paper. Grease the paper and the sides of the tin really thoroughly. Pour the marshmallow mixture into the tin and press into the shape of the tin with a greased spatula.

3. Leave to cool for 10 minutes before cutting into bars. Store in an airtight container for up to a week.

✴ *Raw* ✴
CASHEW CAROB BARS

 MAKES 14

Another raw recipe that is so quick and easy – all you need is a food processor for these delicious power bars. Great for snacking or while on a hike or biking a wooded trail.

135g raw cashew nuts, plus 14 halves for decorating

320g dried dates

45g carob chips

2 teaspoons coconut oil

1 teaspoon lemon juice

3 teaspoons light agave nectar

95g dried unsweetened shredded coconut

1. Using a food processor, process the cashew nuts until finely ground. Pour into a bowl and set aside.

2. Process the dates, carob chips, coconut oil, lemon juice, agave nectar and coconut in the food processor on a high speed for 4 minutes. Stop and scrape down the side of the bowl as needed. Add the ground cashews and process again for 2 minutes, or until the ingredients form a paste.

3. Shape into 7.5cm bars and place a cashew half on top of each. Store in the refrigerator for up to 3 days.

RASPBERRY CHOCOLATE BARS

This is my version of a kicked-up linzer cookie. The addition of chocolate and pecans adds a rich depth of flavour to a deliciously sweet raspberry jam cookie. I also love the addition of oats.

195g unbleached plain flour

160g soft dark brown sugar

1 teaspoon baking powder

225g butter substitute

120g quick-cook oats

45g dried unsweetened shredded coconut

60g shelled pecan nuts, chopped

350g raspberry jam

90g dairy-free and gluten-free chocolate chips

1. Preheat the oven to 180°C/350°F/Gas Mark 4. Grease and flour an 20 x 20cm baking tin.

2. Using a stand mixer, combine the flour, brown sugar and baking powder on a medium speed. With the motor still running, add the butter substitute in tablespoons every 10 seconds until the mixture resembles coarse sand. Add the oats, coconut and pecans. Press one third of the dough into the prepared baking tin. Spoon the jam on top of the dough and sprinkle with the chocolate chips. Place the remaining dough on top.

3. Bake for 25–30 minutes, until bubbly and golden brown. Cool in the baking tin on a wire rack for 30 minutes, then cut into diamond-shaped bars in the tin and serve.

CHOCOLATE PEANUT BUTTER BARS

 MAKES 16

Here is my vegan – and healthier – version of a peanut butter bar. Not only is it delicious, but it's no-bake, so it's quick and easy too!

PEANUT LAYER

280g organic icing sugar

14 Agave Digestive Biscuits (page 104), finely crushed

260g natural unsweetened peanut butter

115g butter substitute, at room temperature

3 tablespoons water

CHOCOLATE LAYER

180g dairy-free and gluten-free chocolate chips

85g butter substitute

1. FIRST MAKE THE PEANUT LAYER. Using a stand mixer, combine the icing sugar and crushed digestive biscuits. Add the peanut butter, butter substitute and water and mix for 1 minute on a medium speed. The mixture will be very thick. Press it into a foil-lined, 20 x 20cm baking tin and set aside.

2. NEXT MAKE THE CHOCOLATE LAYER. In a microwave-safe bowl, combine the chocolate chips and butter substitute. Melt in the microwave for 30–45 seconds, checking to make sure that the chocolate doesn't melt completely. Remove from the microwave and stir the chocolate mixture until it is completely melted.

3. Spoon the chocolate layer on top of the peanut layer and spread evenly. Chill in the refrigerator for 1 hour before cutting into 5cm squares.

✳ Everything Sweet ✳
In Between

✳ RECIPE LIST ✳

Gluten-Free BAKED APPLES

 SERVES 4

This is one of my new favourites. For this filling, you can mix any dried fruit combinations you like, such as cherries and apricots, peaches and raisins, strawberries and blueberries – the possibilities are endless. These are great served warm straight out of the oven.

4 large firm apples
40g soft dark brown sugar
1 teaspoon ground cinnamon
40g sultanas
30g dried cranberries
30g shelled pecan nuts, chopped
4 tablespoons butter substitute
180ml water

1. Preheat the oven to 190°C/375°F/Gas Mark 5.

2. Wash and dry the apples. Using a melon baller, remove the core of the apples to 1cm from the base. Make a hole at the top of each apple 2.5cm wide.

3. In a mixing bowl, combine the brown sugar, cinnamon, sultanas, cranberries and pecans. Stuff each apple with a quarter of the mixture. Top each apple with 1 tablespoon of the butter substitute. Place the apples in a 20 x 20cm baking tin.

4. In a microwave-safe bowl, heat the water in the microwave for 1 minute until it boils. Pour the boiling water into the pan around the apples. Bake for 30–40 minutes, or until the apples are tender but not mushy – the baking time will depend on how large the apples are.

* Raw *
MELON SOUP

 SERVES 4

What a cute way to get our fruit servings for the day. A super-simple recipe with only 4 ingredients (and raw, to boot), it takes no time at all to make. And you can either serve it out of a larger scooped melon or serve it in smaller scooped melons for an extra-special presentation. Serve after dinner before the dessert course.

1 small seedless watermelon
1 small cantaloupe melon
2 tablespoons lemon juice
Fresh mint, for decorating

1. Wash and dry the melons and cut each in half. Using a melon baller, scoop out 10 large watermelon balls and 10 large cantaloupe balls. Place in a small bowl.

2. Scrape out any remaining watermelon and cantaloupe flesh, reserving all 4 halves of the melons, and blend in a food processor for 1 minute. Add the lemon juice and blend again on a high speed for 4 minutes. Pour the 'soup' into the reserved watermelon and cantaloupe 'bowls'. Add 5 melon balls to each bowl. Decorate with fresh mint.

GRIDDLED FRUIT

 SERVES 10–12

Caramelized fruit is so delicious, especially on a hot summer's day. Instead of barbecuing it, you can use a griddle pan or heavy frying pan and get the same char-grilled effect. Serve with soya whip or Coconut Whipped Cream (see page 13) and a sprig of mint.

2 medium peaches

2 medium plums

550g canned pineapple rings, drained

1 cinnamon stick

120ml light agave nectar

1. Wash and dry the peaches and plums. Cut in half and discard the stones. Place in a bowl and add the pineapple, cinnamon stick and 1 litre cold water. Leave the fruit to soak for 10 minutes.

2. In a large greased griddle pan or heavy-based frying pan, cook the fruit over a medium–high heat, adding the cinnamon stick to the pan after 10 minutes when almost done. Turn the fruit over after 5 minutes.

3. Drizzle the fruit with the agave nectar before serving.

PEPPERMINT BARK

This is one of my mother-in-law's favourites. Placed into decorative bags tied with ribbon, I give it out as a Christmas treat to family.

220g chopped organic peppermint sweets

540g dairy-free and gluten-free chocolate chips, tempered (see page 132)

1. Place the peppermint sweets in a food processor and process on a high speed for about 10 seconds or until crushed into small pieces. Set aside.

2. Pour the tempered chocolate onto a parchment-lined baking sheet and spread into an even layer. Sprinkle the chopped peppermints on top.

3. Once the chocolate has hardened, after about 15 minutes, break it into uneven shapes using your hands. Store in an airtight container for up to 2 months.

TOFFEE SQUARES

Who doesn't like toffee? These squares are so easy – and so sinfully delicious that I have to stop myself from eating the whole tray! This is a great dessert to bring to a party.

2 sleeves saltine or dairy-free plain crackers

225g butter substitute

150g soft light brown sugar

350g dairy-free and gluten-free chocolate chips

1. Preheat the oven to 180°C/350°F/Gas Mark 4.
2. Line a 25 x 38cm baking tray with crackers in a single layer.
3. In a medium saucepan, melt the butter substitute and brown sugar over a low heat. Pour evenly over the crackers and bake for 6–8 minutes.
4. Remove the tray from the oven and sprinkle the chocolate chips over the bubbling toffee squares. Once the chips are melted, spread the chocolate evenly. Leave to cool completely, for about 1 hour, and cut into squares. Store in the refrigerator for up to 7 days.

SPICED PECANS

MAKES 450G

Another classic recipe from my childhood, my mum, grandmum and aunts make these delicious pecans around Thanksgiving and Christmas. Perfect in a Mason jar with a ribbon for a gift, the buttery pecans mixed with cinnamon sugar are to die for.

170g evaporated cane juice

1 teaspoon ground cinnamon

1 teaspoon salt

450g pecan halves

1½ teaspoons egg replacer, whisked with 2 tablespoons warm water

1. Preheat the oven to 110°C/225°F/Gas Mark ¼.

2. In a large bowl, mix together the cane juice, cinnamon and salt.

3. In a small bowl, stir the pecans with the egg replacer. Add to the large bowl and toss well. Spoon into a 23 x 33cm baking tin.

4. Bake for 1 hour, stirring every 15 minutes. Store in a glass jar or airtight container. The pecans can be frozen for up to 6 months.

PRETZEL RODS

A very popular dessert at my retail kiosks, the sweet and salty mix of pretzels and chocolate is so tasty. The combinations are endless when making these, as you can see from the 3 different toppings below. Get creative!

24 pretzel rods

675g dairy-free and gluten-free chocolate chips, tempered (see page 132)

105g dairy-free chocolate sandwich biscuits, finely chopped

95g dried unsweetened shredded coconut

240g dried cranberries

125g shelled pistachio nuts, chopped

1. Have your bowl of tempered chocolate at hand. Take a large piece of foil or greaseproof paper and line your work surface. Make separate piles of each topping: the finely chopped biscuits, the coconut, the dried cranberries and the chopped pistachios.

2. Dip 2 pretzel rods together at the same time into the bowl of chocolate and, using an offset spatula, spread the chocolate onto the rods, making sure to leave 2.5cm at the top of the pretzels for a handle. Remove any excess chocolate.

3. Place the chocolate-dipped pretzel rods onto the topping of your choice. Cover the entire chocolate part of the pretzel with the topping and then transfer to the piece of foil or greaseproof paper to dry. Repeat with all the pretzel rods and toppings.

4. The pretzel rods will keep for 2 months in an airtight container.

TEMPERING CHOCOLATE AND MAKING CHOCOLATE CUPS

Once you have mastered the principles of tempering chocolate you can make so many great desserts. Like these chocolate mousse cups – super-easy and everyone will ask, 'How did you do that?'

Small saucepan

Medium stainless-steel bowl

720g dairy-free and gluten-free chocolate chips

Large piece of foil or greaseproof paper

5 small round balloons

1. First add 240ml water to the small saucepan and bring it to a simmer over a medium heat. Place 540g of the chocolate chips in the stainless-steel bowl and place the bowl on top of the simmering pan. Stir the chocolate constantly until it is 80% melted. Take the bowl off the pan and dry the base of it, making sure that no water gets into the melted chocolate. Continue stirring the chocolate off the heat until it has completely melted.

2. Add the remaining 180g chocolate chips and stir until melted. The more you stir the better. This agitates the crystals in the chocolate and allows the chocolate to dry quickly and snap when you bite into it.

3. Once all of the chocolate is melted, test it with your finger. If the chocolate is cool to the touch, put a small amount on a piece of foil. If it hardens and is shiny within 2–3 minutes, it is in temper. If it doesn't harden, continue to stir and add another 25g chocolate, stirring, until it is melted. Repeat until the chocolate is in temper.

4. Blow up all 5 balloons and dip each into the tempered chocolate. Shake each balloon after dipping to remove excess chocolate. Place on a parchment-lined baking sheet and leave to dry for about 10 minutes. Once dry, pop the balloons with a knife and remove each balloon from the base of each cup.

5. The cups can now be filled with Chocolate Mousse (see page 134) or Coconut Whipped Cream (see page 13) and fresh fruit.

CHOCOLATE MOUSSE

My delicious chocolate mousse is made with melted chocolate for a rich and decadent flavour. Spoon or pipe into chocolate cups and serve with fresh raspberries and mint for a very easy but beautiful dessert for a special occasion.

800g silken tofu, cubed and drained

360g dairy-free and gluten-free chocolate chips

225g tofu cream cheese, at room temperature

115g tofu sour cream

140g organic icing sugar

¼ teaspoon xanthan gum (optional)

5 Chocolate Cups (see page 132)

1. In a food processor, process the tofu on a high speed for 3 minutes, stopping and scraping down the side of the bowl every minute, or until the tofu is creamy in texture. Meanwhile, melt the chocolate in a microwave-safe bowl in the microwave at 75% power for about 1 minute 30 seconds until softened, stopping and stirring after each 30-second interval. Turn the food processor to a low speed and pour the melted chocolate into the bowl. Mix for 2 minutes, stopping and scraping down the side of the bowl, until well combined.

2. Using a stand mixer, beat the cream cheese for about 1 minute until smooth. Stop and scrape down the side of the bowl. Add the sour cream, icing sugar and xanthan gum, if using. Mix on a medium-high speed for 1 minute. Add the chocolate tofu mixture to the bowl and blend on a high speed for 1 minute.

3. Cover with cling film and refrigerate the chocolate mousse for 30 minutes before piping into the chocolate cups. The mousse will keep for 1 week in the refrigerator.

TIRAMISU

Tiramisu means 'pick me up' in Italian. In my vegan version, I use Marsala instead of rum, which adds such a nice flavour. I sell this in restaurants and most people don't even know it's vegan and they love it. The alternating layers and flavours go together so well.

225g butter substitute, at room temperature

255g evaporated cane juice

2 teaspoons vanilla extract

390g unbleached plain flour

4 teaspoons baking powder

6 teaspoons egg replacer, whisked with 8 tablespoons warm water

240ml soya milk

1 tablespoon cider vinegar

COFFEE FILLING

480ml strong black coffee

60ml Marsala

Cream Cheese Frosting (page 66)

Shaved dairy-free chocolate, for sprinkling

1. Preheat the oven to 180°C/350°F/Gas Mark 4. Grease and flour a 25 x 38cm baking tray or shallow baking tin.

2. Using a stand mixer, beat together the butter substitute, cane juice and vanilla extract on a medium speed until combined. Stop and scrape down the side of the bowl, increase the speed to high and beat the mixture for about 2 minutes until light and fluffy

3. In a small bowl, combine the flour and baking powder. In a separate bowl, mix together the egg replacer, soya milk and vinegar. Alternate adding the dry and wet ingredients to the mixer bowl, starting and ending with the dry ingredients,, beating for 10 seconds after each addition. Stop and scrape down side of bowl, making sure that all the butter substitute is incorporated. Beat for 30 seconds on a medium speed. Spread the mixture evenly onto the prepared baking sheet.

4. Bake the cake for 20–25 minutes, or until a wooden skewer inserted in the centre of the cake comes out clean. Cool the tin on a wire rack for 10 minutes, then flip the tin over to release the cake. Leave to cool for a further 45 minutes.

5. While the cake is baking, brew the coffee. Leave to cool, then add the Marsala. Set aside.

6. Once the cake has cooled, cut it into 3 even sections. Place the first layer on a serving plate and prick it all over with a fork. Using a pastry brush, liberally dab the coffee mixture onto the cake. Spread over a third of the Cream Cheese Frosting and sprinkle with chocolate shavings. Repeat 2 more times. Store the tiramisu in the refrigerator for up to 5 days.

CHOCOLATE STRAWBERRY TRIFLE

 SERVES 4

This features an alternative to my chocolate mousse using a vegan chocolate mousse mix. Combine with strawberries, chocolate digestive biscuit crust and chocolate drizzle for a luxurious treat.

DIGESTIVE BISCUIT CRUST

24 Chocolate Digestive Biscuits (page 102)

45g evaporated cane juice

115g butter substitute

CHOCOLATE FILLING

400g firm tofu

25g cocoa powder, sifted

120g packet dairy-free and gluten-free chocolate mousse dessert mix

115g tofu sour cream

6 tablespoons soya milk, plus extra if needed

290g hulled strawberries

180g dairy-free and gluten-free chocolate chips, melted

1. FIRST MAKE THE CRUST. In a food processor, finely crush the chocolate digestive biscuits for about 2 minutes. Place in a medium bowl and add the cane juice. In a microwave-safe bowl, melt the butter substitute in the microwave for about 30 seconds. Add to the biscuit crumb mixture, stir and set aside.

2. NEXT MAKE THE CHOCOLATE FILLING. Using a food processor, process the tofu for about 2 minutes until smooth, stopping and scraping down the side of the bowl as necessary. Add the cocoa powder, chocolate mousse mix, sour cream and soya milk. Process on a high speed for 2 minutes until well combined, adding extra soya milk if the mixture is a little too thick.

3. Wash and dry the strawberries, then cut into 5mm-thick slices. Set aside.

4. Using glass serving dishes, alternate layering the digestive biscuit crust with the chocolate filling and strawberries. Top each trifle with some drizzled melted chocolate.

RESOURCES

MAGAZINES

The Vegan
A quarterly magazine published by The Vegan Society, available throughout the UK in all good health food stores and free to various groups and organisations (upon request) and all paid members of the Vegan Society. It is also available from their online shop.
www.vegansociety.com

Vegan Views
A magazine run by volunteers since the 70s, *Vegan Views* started life as a newsletter produced by a group of young vegans living in London, who wanted to make contact and share news and opinions with others who were interested in creating a more harmonious way of living based on veganism.
www.veganviews.org.uk

ANIMAL ADVOCACY GROUPS

Farm Sanctuary
Farm Sanctuary is an American animal protection organisation, founded in 1986 (and originally funded by sales of vegetarian hot dogs at Grateful Dead concerts) as an advocate for farm animals. It promotes laws and policies that support animal welfare, animal protection and vegetarianism/veganism by rescue, education and advocacy. Farm Sanctuary houses over 800 cows, chickens, ducks, geese, turkeys, pigs, sheep, rabbits and goats at a 70-hectare animal sanctuary in Watkins Glen, New York.
www.farmsanctuary.org

RSPCA
The Royal Society for the Prevention of Cruelty to Animals was established in 1824 with a vision to work for a world in which all humans respect and live in harmony with all other members of the animal kingdom. It works with the government and public to prevent cruelty and prosecutes those who neglect the law, on behalf of defenceless animals.
www.rspca.org

Viva
Viva! believes that eating meat; fish and dairy causes environmental destruction, damages human health, contributes to global hunger and inflicts immense suffering on billions of animals across the world and that the solution to all these problems is in our own hands.
www.viva.org.uk

One Kind
OneKind, formerly Advocates for Animals, is a UK-based animal charity and a movement of people who live an animal-friendly lifestyle as the mainstream; in the same way that green living and recycling or Fairtrade are now mainstream lifestyle choices for millions of people.
www.onekind.org

Animal Aid
Animal Aid is the UK's largest animal rights group and campaigns peacefully against all forms of animal abuse to promote a cruelty-free lifestyle.
www.animalaid.org

NUTRITION & MEETING RESOURCES

The Vegetarian Resource Group
Covers vegan nutrition (including calcium, iron, protein and vitamins D and B12).
www.vrg.org

Vegan Society
A range of advice on maintaining a healthy, well-planned vegan diet.
www.vegansociety.com

EarthSave
Founded by 'Diet for a New America' author John Robbins. A non-profit, educational organisation promoting awareness of the health, environmental and ethical consequences of food choices.
www.earthsave.org

Goodness Direct
Eco and organic shopping, covering food, health, beauty and household cleaning products.
www.goodnessdirect.co.uk

Dietary Needs Direct
Offering healthy and natural foods and products for an additive- and synthetic-free lifestyle.
www.dietaryneedsdirect.co.uk

BOOKS

Fast Food Nation by Eric Schlosser, Harper Perennial, 2002

Skinny Bitch by Rory Freedman and Kim Barnouin, Running Press, 2005
www.skinnybitch.net

Vegan in 30 Days by Sarah Taylor, Taylor Presentations, 2008

✳ INDEX ✳

✳ ACKNOWLEDGMENTS ✳

I am so grateful to my Mum and Grandmum for showing me their love of baking and sharing it with me. I know they would be so proud of my accomplishments.

To my husband Paul, for his never-ending support and encouragement. Without you I wouldn't be where I am today.

To Gene, for all that you do for animals. Your tireless work on behalf of those who do not have their own voices is such an inspiration. I hope to be like you and give my all to better the treatment of all animals.

To Anja, your support and patience has made this experience so great. Thank you for believing in me and my desserts.